FATHERS

A COLLECTION OF POEMS

Other Books by David Ray

X-Rays: A Book of Poems
Dragging the Main and Other Poems
Gathering Firewood: New Poems and Selected
Enough of Flying: Poems Inspired by the Ghazals of Ghalib
The Mulberries of Mingo and Other Stories
The Tramp's Cup
The Touched Life
Not Far From the River
On Wednesday I Cleaned Out My Wallet
Elysium in the Halls of Hell
Sam's Book
The Maharani's New Wall
Wool Highways
Kangaroo Paws: Poems Written in Australia

Other Books Edited

The Chicago Review Anthology
From the Hungarian Revolution
A Poetry Reading Against the Vietnam War (with Robert Bly)
Richard Wright: Impressions and Perspectives (with Robert Farnsworth)
New Asian Writing (with Judy Ray)
The Jack Conroy Reader (with Jack Salzman)
From A to Z: 200 American Poets
The Collected Poems of E. L. Mayo
New Letters Reader I and II
India: An Anthology of Contemporary Writing (with Amritjit Singh)

Other Books by Judy Ray

Pebble Rings
The Jaipur Sketchbook: Impressions of India
Pigeons in the Chandeliers

FATHERS

A COLLECTION OF POEMS

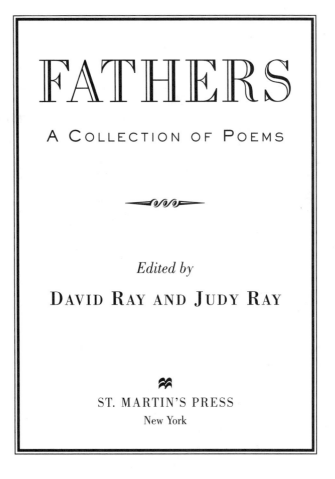

Edited by

DAVID RAY AND JUDY RAY

ST. MARTIN'S PRESS
New York

FATHERS: A COLLECTION OF POEMS. Copyright © 1997 by David Ray and Judy Ray. All rights reserved. Printed in the United States of America. No part of this book may be used or reproduced in any manner whatsoever without written permission except in the case of brief quotations embodied in critical articles or reviews. For information, address St. Martin's Press, 175 Fifth Avenue, New York, N.Y. 10010.

Production Editor: David Stanford Burr

Design: Jennifer Ann Daddio

Library of Congress Cataloging-in-Publication Data

Fathers : a collection of poems / edited by David Ray and Judy Ray. —
    1st ed.
            p.   cm.
        ISBN 0-312-15527-1
        1. Fathers—Poetry.   2. American poetry—20th century.   I. Ray,
    David.   II. Ray, Judy.
    PS595.F39F38   1997
    811.008'03520431—dc21   96-54504
                                                              CIP

First Edition: June 1997

10 9 8 7 6 5 4 3 2 1

Contents

INTRODUCTION

When we cast about for poems about fathers, we found no shortage. Every poet has a poem about the remembered father—loved, hated, admired, resented. Our focus at first was the "missing" father, for if our country is not "Fatherless America," it is at least a troubled America when it comes to discussions of fatherhood. And it seems that in the most prosperous nation in the world happy families—or at least happy relationships with fathers—are rare. Tolstoy's famous remark about happy families all being alike, while "every unhappy family is unhappy in its own way" might today be tailored to target fathers.

To recall a father is often to awaken old traumas, relive arguments, resuffer grief. Rarely is there not much to forgive at a deathbed. "The happy man leaves no record," Samuel Butler told us, and therefore we held out some hope that only certain writers carry such bitterness, while others are surely free of it. Not wanting to present a book that was only a tribute to survival of abuse, neglect, and dysfunction, we sought writers who *were* free of it. We tilted the configuration of our net to draw in other voices and more varied views from contemporary poets in America. And we, the editors, also bring different personal experiences to this theme, David having known a broken home and the absence of a father, Judy having grown up on an English farm with the steady, loyal presence of both parents.

Not only are the views varied, they are ever changing, as fathers are experienced over time and through the refractions of advancing age. Like Mark Twain, some writers find themselves surprised at how much a father has learned over the years. As awareness grows that he was not the monolith once perceived as unshakable, but a person who had emerged from his own childhood, perception of a father wavers like images through telescopes that can reach back and gather light from a time anterior to ours. Some poets can thus share memories not only of their own childhoods, but of their fathers' earliest hopes and losses.

Often the absence of a father made him a figure even more vivid than one whose gifts of presence and nurture were positive. Both physical and emotional distance can leave "a hole in the world" of a child, and more than one poet has undertaken the daunting task of describing that hole in the world. Yet the father may be wronged by the accusation that he has treated the children as regrettable detritus to be left behind or as coconspirators with ex-wives. He is, after all, a tissue of dreams and longings as well as of memorable realities, shaped of polymorphic clay and, in some cases, broken promises or such profound differences as to make the two generations seem like representatives of different species.

To know one's father and to know him accurately is a central goal of every life, and we project that goal into our politics, our workplace, and our struggles within ourselves. Many of us who strive to understand our fathers—mysterious indeed if they were largely absent—and then became fathers ourselves have come to know the pain felt from the father's side of the abyss as well. And those with positive feelings must nevertheless endure the separation of death, the affliction of mourning.

The script never changes, R. D. Laing told us, only the players. Without good role models we have little chance of becoming good parents ourselves. Our efforts are frequently undermined by a culture that pressures fathers to become irrelevant in their children's lives. When there is no incentive other than love for the child, that love may turn to grief, as in F. Scott Fitzgerald's powerful story "Babylon Revisited," where a loving father is judged by a harsh and distorted dredging up of his past.

Thus inheritance of traits is a theme addressed by many of our poets. Parents are introjected early in life, with the result that we are, in a sense, our fathers and mothers, and the inner child lives on as well. The family pattern itself, the script, is legacy, with all its karmic compulsions and lures. Even the disavowed father is there somewhere, inside his child. And some poets, like Paul Mariani with his Dantesque vision, can imagine both their fathers and themselves in hell.

Fathers as heroes and antiheroes, as abusers and defenders, as victims and persecutors, men who regarded their children as treasures or as nuisances, those who disappeared and those who reappeared, those who were always there and those who were never there—are all here, in this roundup of poems chosen not only for what they say but for their emotional power and aesthetic achievement. The poems here may seldom fit Wordsworth's "emotion recollected in tranquillity" because of the rareness of tranquillity. But they more often meet Randall Jarrell's idea of the poet standing in a storm and being hit by lightning. Our poets have been hit by many lightning bolts (six make a great poet, Jarrell decided). This book, then, might well be compared to an impressive lightning display. Structured elegance or tumbling rockfall, these poems are dangerous. They are alive with disquietude, but not "disquietude for its own sake," which seems to be the case in much contemporary poetry.

Both daughters and sons introduce their fathers to us in this anthology, and several poets share their own joy and sorrow as fathers. The forms they choose for their writing are varied, too, ranging from free verse to prose poem, sestina to villanelle. Of course, as the poet Qiu Xiaolong reminds us in a note, "a poet's father does not have to be the father in the poem." We also asked our contributors to provide brief information about their fathers—outside the context of a poem—and found ourselves moved to read the acknowledgments of hardworking lives in a variety of careers. Some of those characterizations remind us of George Colman the Younger's nineteenth-century *Sylvester Dagger-wood:* "My father was an eminent button maker—but I had a soul above buttons—I panted for a liberal profession." We wish, of course, we lived in a world where everyone could speak of a remembered father the way Gwendolyn Brooks does.

We regret only that we had to limit our collection. Most of these contributors have far more to say on the subject than they can share here, and there are many compelling works by others we could not include. We hope that this volume will lead to further exploration of the theme with your reading of these and other poets. We'd like to hear from you—about your fathers—and about your experience of this book.

Our special thanks go to friends who discussed our project with us in helpful ways or nudged us to consider the merits of a poem we might have overlooked. Those friends include many of the poets in this volume as well as Mary and Michael Cuddihy, James P. Hepburn, Vernon "Bud" Rowe, Amritjit Singh, and others.

Most of all, we thank our children for teaching us the joys and perils of parenthood, whether it be as biological, adoptive, or stepparents. Loving, striving, struggling, never giving up are the common burden and privilege.

—DAVID RAY AND JUDY RAY

THE OLIVE WOOD FIRE

When Fergus woke crying at night
I would carry him from his crib
to the rocking chair and sit holding him
before the fire of thousand-year-old olive wood,
which it took a quarter-hour of matches
and kindling to get burning right. Sometimes
—for reasons I never knew and he has forgotten—
even after his bottle the big tears
would keep on rolling down his big cheeks
—the left cheek always more brilliant than the right—
and we would sit, some nights for hours,
rocking in the almost lightless light
eking itself out of the ancient wood,
and hold each other against the darkness,
his close behind and far away in the future,
mine I imagined all around.
One such time, fallen half-asleep myself,
I thought I heard a scream
—a flier crying out in horror
as he dropped fire on he didn't know what or whom,
or else a child thus set aflame—
and sat up alert. The olive wood fire
had burned low. In my arms lay Fergus,
fast asleep, left cheek glowing, God.

1

WILLIAM STAFFORD

A Story That Could Be True

If you were exchanged in the cradle and
your real mother died
without ever telling the story
then no one knows your name,
and somewhere in the world
your father is lost and needs you
but you are far away.

He can never find
how true you are, how ready.
When the great wind comes
and the robberies of the rain
you stand on the corner shivering.
The people who go by—
you wonder at their calm.

They miss the whisper that runs
any day in your mind,
"Who are you really, wanderer?"—
and the answer you have to give
no matter how dark and cold
the world around you is:
"Maybe I'm a king."

AFTER THE QUIET RAIN

Finding the true word which creates us is like finding the parents,
  the solitude is not literary though we can think of it
  as a long novel, novelty that keeps us
  going across the desert or across the
  ocean until
we find the parents who are about to get their script from
  motions of the galaxy and about to
  make love which creates us;
this dim May morning I walk by wet magnolia blossoms
  and the simple wet truth of forsythia.

STAMP

My father collected stamps, cutting
days and nights to small squares,
soaking a sky full of them
in a washbasin, and drying them
on the doors, windows, and mirrors:
two stamps in his eyes,
the face an unfamiliar envelope,
the world an unfolding album.

I, too, was glued onto a piece
of white paper. The snow was falling,
a message in each flake; a crane's
footprint disappeared overnight.
Mailed to a nonexistent address
to possess a postmark, I was not
returned, as it occasionally happens,
by a mistake at the post office.

THE TRESTLE

I've wasted my time this morning, and I'm deeply ashamed.
I went to bed last night thinking about my dad.
About that little river we used to fish—Butte Creek—
near Lake Almanor. Water lulled me to sleep.
In my dream, it was all I could do not to get up
and move around. But when I woke early this morning
I went to the telephone instead. Even though
the river was flowing down there in the valley,
in the meadows, moving through ditch clover.
Fir trees stood on both sides of the meadows. And I was there.
A kid sitting on a timber trestle, looking down.
Watching my dad drink from his cupped hands.
Then he said, "This water's so good.
I wish I could give my mother some of this water."
My dad still loved her, though she was dead
and he'd been away from her for a long time.
He had to wait some more years
until he could go where she was. But he loved
this country where he found himself. The West.
For thirty years it had him around the heart,
and then it let him go. He went to sleep one night
in a town in northern California
and didn't wake up. What could be simpler?

I wish my own life, and death, could be so simple.
So that when I woke on a fine morning like this,
after being somewhere I wanted to be all night,
somewhere important, I could move most naturally
and without thinking about it, to my desk.

Say I did that, in the simple way I've described.
From bed to desk back to childhood.
From there it's not so far to the trestle.
And from the trestle I could look down
and see my dad when I needed to see him.
My dad drinking that cold water. My sweet father.
The river, its meadows, and firs, and the trestle.
That. Where I once stood.

I wish I could do that
without having to plead with myself for it.
And feel sick of myself
for getting involved in lesser things.
I know it's time I changed my life.
This life—the one with its complications
and phone calls—is unbecoming,
and a waste of time.
I want to plunge my hands in clear water. The way
he did. Again and then again.

EASTER

My father was a warrior, he wore the white
dress with red vest, fez, tufted
hobnailed shoes. He danced
Fred Astaire-thin, on tiptoe led the line
of skirted men to power. Pipe fiddle drum, he charmed a gun
asleep, he heard his mother
once or twice yell *Nicholas!* and turned
quickfooted as the bullet
missed. He dreamed
his mother up through me, his *brujo* dream. He raised her,
dancing pleats a flash, red vest, red head, red shoes eggs wine,
the gyring spitted lamb, so long
he danced, so slow she rose, she rose and crossed
my eyes that saw him split in midair impossibly and hold
        her, hold me close.

In Honor of David Anderson Brooks, My Father

July 30, 1883–November 21, 1959

A dryness is upon the house
My father loved and tended.
Beyond his firm and sculptured door
His light and lease have ended.

He walks the valleys, now—replies
To sun and wind forever.
No more the cramping chamber's chill,
No more the hindering fever.

Now out upon the wide clean air
My father's soul revives,
All innocent of self-interest
And the fear that strikes and strives.

He who was Goodness, Gentleness,
And Dignity is free,
Translates to public Love
Old private charity.

THICK AS HONEST MEMORY

My father's thick hand holds mine
and I his.
We are wind chill 18 degrees one hungry lung
who must believe our lives against this war.

Mother stands apart inside the glass doors
hiding from cold,
her thin body stiff as all the barricaded words.
Trouble is, she says, *we can't make a difference.*
Nothing will change.

My father's hand in mine does trust
a sudden shift in weather
his fingers thick as honey, honest memory.

Years I have leaned into his holding
against all language of shame.
Today's paper says six hundred
but we know that many thousands gather here
protesting unjust war. Between our touching fingertips.

ONCE

"Mother, what is Labor Day?" I once
asked. "That, my dear, is when everybody

else in the country goes to the beach
except us," she said over her heavy iron,

her heavy irony. Why everybody else,
not us? Was there a national lottery?

Had our family, like blind Pew, drawn
the black spot? If not this year, could we

go the next? It was years before I understood.
One year we went to the beach. A new world,

half an hour away. I never had seen
the ocean. My big toe in the Atlantic!

Mother and the four of us on the beach,
Father on the boardwalk on a bench,

under an umbrella, wearing a ratty straw hat.
Suddenly he was somebody's old aunt!

(Once he'd gotten sun poisoning fishing,
he claimed.) He looked at his wristwatch a lot.

Mother wore an ancient wool bathing suit,
her legs thin as the stork's.

I leapt repeatedly into the muscled sea,
the sea rumpled, my brothers romped,

the sun felt good, the salt smelt good,
Jesus! it was fun, and we never went back.

FATHER'S DAY

When I was eight you put me
on the Sky-Line roller coaster at Riverside
where I screamed all day
holding to a steel bar
unable to get off.
While you were shaking dice behind a tent,
I was rising and falling,
a strip of tickets crumpled in my hand.
In 1950 you were reading Epictetus late at night
falling asleep in your chair.
Years earlier you wrote in your diary,
"New girl in town. Quinn and I
had a shot at her."
Sitting in the orchestra pit
drumming the pratfalls,
the vaudeville timed to your wrist rolls.
My first groom. Mother was shy.
She said I could not marry you.
She kept me for myself.
She did not know the wet lips
you kissed me with one morning.
What an irritable man you were.
Rising and falling,

I could not remember who I was.
Whole summers consumed
in the sound of glass wind chimes.
When you died they scattered your ashes in a field.
At any moment I can breathe in the burned powder of your body,
the bitter taste, the residue.

LEARNING ON OLMSTEAD STREET

The tattoo of a heart with an arrow
piercing it has MOTHER written in blue
across the pink center, and it moves
each time my father piles another stack
of coins on the kitchen table or reaches
to lift the gold glass of beer. Who
was the sixth president, he asks, the capital
of Idaho, Nebraska, what's the difference
between the Arctic and Antarctic, the change
for two boxes of doughnuts at twenty-three
cents each if the man hands me a five-
dollar bill? Even as I stand to wrap
sandwiches in wax paper, folding
the corners in neat triangles the way
he taught me, he asks the names
of the last three governors of New York,
says in French I've dropped the knife.
Bending to pick it up, he's suddenly
beside me, his eyes bloodshot,
his breath blue smoke as he repeats
the average life span of an ant, a moth,
then wipes up the stain in looping
figure eights, the sign for infinity
he says, tossing me the dirty cloth.

HARDWARE

My father always knew the secret
name of everything—
stove bolt and wing nut,
set screw and rasp, ratchet
wrench, band saw, and ball-
peen hammer. He was my
tour guide and translator
through that foreign country
with its short-tempered natives
in their crewcuts and tattoos,
who suffered my incompetence
with gruffness and disgust.
Pay attention, he would say,
and you'll learn a thing or two.

Now it's forty years later,
and I'm packing up his tools
(*If you know the proper
names of things you're never
at a loss*) tongue-tied, incompetent,
my hands and heart full
of doohickeys and widgets,
whatchamacallits, thingamabobs.

JUDITH VOLLMER

FATHER'S MAGIC TRICK

He could grab the hot casserole and dance
the kitchen with it while we clapped
and squealed at him never to put it down.
"I have hot hands," he'd sing and laugh
at supper in the early Sixties
when I pretended I was the meteor girl

who stood beside him leaning over the pool
inside the nuclear dome where he worked
adjusting fuel rods like pickup sticks
to stoke the fire that meant
heat, light & wealth for us all.

He worked with his hands tying
fuel bundles in the chambers of Fermi & Chalk River.
His hands were thick as oven mitts,
safe enough after touching the atomic fire
to touch anything. Down in the cellar
welding toys & lawnchairs bare-handed
he always had an audience at the window,
kids peering in at the strobes
watching him bend over his
blue flame & wand.

16

THE BICYCLE

The bicycle disconsolate for decades
among used lumber in the garage rafters
lies embedded in its year—fifteen—
which I can never let go, which is
no litter of the past, but myself
on the rim of the horizon
when the walls of my father's house fell open
and I was outside, everywhere on my own.

WAKING TO THE COMET

You were beside me.
You were the mountain
blocking half
a sky full of stars.

I was small
in the depth of your shadow,
watching black water
and glittering boats.

Everyone sat
on blankets in grass,
drinking and eating,
talking and waiting.

I played, then slept,
until your hand stirred me.
I woke among strangers
all staring up.

High overhead,
faint, among whispers,

floated a figure
with long glowing hair.

You called it by name.
Everyone watched it.
I watched you and mother,
the way your cheeks shone.

Once in a lifetime, you said,
soft as breathing,
speaking to no one.
I loved you both then.

I saw mother, crying,
the way her hand glowed
through darkness toward
the ghost of your hand.

Now I am grown.
You've gone to earth.
I have my own child,
and the comet we saw

is just starting back
from a distance much deeper
than I could have guessed
as a boy in the gathering dew.

Prayer

for my father

When you were ten,
your life depended
on the single glow of a cigarette.
It was the way your mother's
hired guide signaled to each of you—
to run from one ancient tomb
to another, as you panicked,
in inches of stops and starts
past the city of Haeju,
thirty-eighth parallel, North Korea,
1944. Overhead, crossing arms of light
swept the upper lip of this bay,
coming so close, at times,
to your tomb,
that you must have hugged
the rough stone with gratitude,
the whiskers of grass
against your face. Unable to cry.
Were there sirens? Fog?
Nothing, in fact, would blur you
from the one, steady proof
flaring briefly, and only once,

20

that what sounded like your
footfalls were your brother's
running ahead,
that behind you, your sister would fit
into the bent palm your body made,
and after her, a half mile or more away,
your mother would crouch
in this same place.
All the while, thick searchlights
full of men's voices
pummeled toward you
in the middle of the night. Later,
you would not remember running at all.
Only the enormous stones
you held, arms flattened on either side
of you, as you waited—young as you were—
for the small mouth of burn
to open in the cupped
hands of distance. Unable to breathe.
How you would open your eyes
every morning for the rest of your life
and speak first to God.
I want to tell you
that my life depends
on imagining
your hard boy feet, the way
they hit below sea grass,
below the packed sand that lies

the other side of this world,
in the grit of my heart.
I know how the heart grows
from running like this,
filling the clenched fists,
the desire to continue
toward that small fire pulsing,
that sometimes means shutting
out the mind
and living by signal,
eyes closed.

GRAPE SHERBET

The day? Memorial.
After the grill
Dad appears with his masterpiece—
swirled snow, gelled light.
We cheer. The recipe's
a secret and he fights
a smile, his cap turned up
so the bib resembles a duck.

That morning we galloped
through the grassed-over mounds
and named each stone
for a lost milk tooth. Each dollop
of sherbet, later,
is a miracle,
like salt on a melon that makes it sweeter.

Everyone agrees—it's wonderful!
It's just how we imagined lavender
would taste. The diabetic grandmother
stares from the porch,
a torch
of pure refusal.

We thought no one was lying
there under our feet,
we thought it
was a joke. I've been trying
to remember the taste,
but it doesn't exist.
Now I see why
you bothered,
father.

NAILS

My father, his mouth full of nails,
is building my mother's dream house.

My mother is listing the grief
it cost her, & pointing out how smooth

the woodwork is. To her brothers:
well, the blacks are taking over—

& her cousins passing through from Santa Monica
swear the church is kissing ass. Ah,

a dream house draws the line on many
fronts. (St. Monica, if I remember, wed thou thee

a pagan, no? & brought him in the fold.
& when he died thou set

to work on sonny boy, old dissolute Augustine, right?
Any food in there for thought?)

Meanwhile, time to pour
the basement floor,

& the Ready Mix man plops
his concrete through the future

rec room window, *Lord*
it isn't wet enough to spread!

Just lays there like a load some giant chicken
dropped. My father, mixing figures,

says all hell will hit the fan
if our fannies do not *move*

& sets my little brother on it with the hose
while we grab hoes & shovels. Lord

I liked that part & afterwards
the lump all smooth

we drank our beer & pop
& mopped our sweat,

& talked about What Next.
The future meant:

cut the lumber square,
make the nails go straight

& things will hold.
I loved that logic, saw him prove it—

then he said we're done
& covered up the last nail's head

with wood paste;
everything was smooth.

I moved around a lot
when I left home, making stories up.

In one blockbuster there's a lady says:
"You taste like roofing nails, father."

And: "You're growing shorter!"
Terrific dialogue but not much plot.

Like building dream houses—
no one knows what you mean.

"MORE LIGHT!"

—Goethe

Suppose those last words
were not a desperate request
but a stunned exclamation,
death a door flung open
into a dark that dazzled
like sun on water.

And what of those other last words,
unfamous in the dry mouth
of an aunt after surgery,
someone holding her papery hand;
or the stranger pulled
from the roadside wreck?

What of those dying alone,
their revelations spoken into emptiness,
into air, the way my father died
at the foot of the hill
below his garden of blueberries?

In the years since his death,
I've remembered those times

the house went dark and he
stumbled blind down basement stairs,
nothing visible, not even his feet
lifted beneath him like flippers under water,
and my mother called from above him
where we all huddled together
to ask if he was all right,
and suddenly the air was luminous.

A LITTLE BIT OF SOAP

One of the things my father never liked about me was my dark skin. *You used to be so pretty* was the way he'd put it, and it was true, there is proof, a baby picture of a curly-haired, just a hair's breadth away from fair-skinned child, me, my small fingers balled up into fists.

And then, as if some God shrugged and suddenly turned away its gaze, something caved in, and I was dark, dark, and all that it implied.

So what happened? My father always seemed to want me to explain, what did this desertion mean? This skin that seemed born to give up, this hair that crinkled to knots, this fairy tale-like transformation?

You used to look real good, my father, a man of slightly lighter hue, would say to me, his son, his changeling. *Maybe you ought to wash more.*

SNOW

Late December: my father and I
are going to New York, to the circus.
He holds me
on his shoulders in the bitter wind:
scraps of white paper
blow over the railroad ties.

My father liked
to stand like this, to hold me
so he couldn't see me.
I remember
staring straight ahead
into the world my father saw;
I was learning
to absorb its emptiness,
the heavy snow
not falling, whirling around us.

Moments with Dad

boxing with dad
I but a child
he, large
though still on his knees
I threw jabs and wild rights
at his face that never
seemed still
I struck air
and the heavy, worked hands
with the black thumbnail

one day of catch
in a park
somewhere in L.A.
a different day
not of work, or hunting
or other families
but catch and throw with him and me

an all-star game
in 1965, summer after 6th grade
I was 12 and he was 33
I circled bases

he snapped pictures
that I never saw
the next one he came to
was 1984, a July in San Francisco
we drank fine white wine
and ate pasta and abalone

silent times in forests
we stalked wildlife, listened
to the quiet
walked our Indian way
with him in the lead
we tried to miss the dry twigs

a duck hunt in Kansas
it was bitter cold
we got one duck
all that a father and son need

a long drive back
to Seattle from Canada
with the best hamburger ever shared
and the mysterious gas tank
that read empty the whole way

OLD TUNES

Oh, where have you been, Billy boy, Billy boy?
I have been to seek a wife; she's the joy of my life . . .

When the road dipped deep
and sky took over the car,
plastering each side of the family 'wagon
with southern Ohio,
and my father's broad grin
caught on the towns of Chillicothe and Portsmouth
while they sucked us in with their steel-mill smoke stacks,
small-town diners, and steeples slanted enough to let
the sun roll down and into the notes
that cluttered the front seat,
we three kids leaned and shoved and grabbed
at my father's songs to make them ours.

Bubbling "Down by the Old Mill Stream,"
we stopped to peel our socks,
wave them at passing trucks,
small prophecies of our victory
as we took the first steps
into the icy wet of his childhood
creek, not once letting go

of the wide hope
of his arm.

And later,
my great aunt's pastry stuck
at the lowest parts of our stomachs,
an awful weight,
we spit out "'Neath the Crust of the Old Apple Pie"
and other melodic jokes
strung on the shaky chords
of my father's voice
from dance halls, summer camps, nights in the navy,
where he dreamed of the slow step
and fingers, smooth as a seductive dance,
that he'd finally find
years later on my mother.

Who was why,
those weeks in the car,
he bellowed and beamed
and zigzagged us into the summers
that smelled and tasted of song:
boogie-woogie and bebop, but mostly the cool blue
of Sinatra and Gershwin,
his one hand gliding across the wheel
the other, over and over throughout our lives,
tapping his syncopated love notes
on the open heart of her palm.

My Father's Living Room

Evening papers
crinkled in his lap,
his hands were clean,
nails trimmed short, his signet ring
had no initial.
I read the headlines from the floor,
trying to see inside, squinting to read
the little letters under the thick ones.
He turned the pages slowly.

"Don't bother your father," my mother
whispered. I learned not to. I practiced
quiet, practiced over and over
scales of silences,
learning as long as I didn't
startle him,
I could make my move
when the paper came down.

As we talked I would shiver
from holding in my words,
from not letting them out
too loudly,

36

from holding my ribs
close as piano keys
so I could sound
his fears.

THE SCIENTIST

Other fathers might cuss out a lawnmower
that wouldn't catch. Or kick the car.
Mine would simply stop. A physicist, he'd stop
and think awhile, his breath wheezing
through his nose—hiss and hiss, mechanical
until, abruptly, a solution clicked.
Then, step by step, arranging parts
in the sequence they'd come loose,
he'd direct at our lawnmower a logic
even that sullen machine could not refute.
Then, just as systematically, refit
each wrench upon its pegboard silhouette,
re-index every drill bit, every nail—
this small, half-German intellectual
who, although he'd own no gun himself,
let me wear twin Lone Ranger cap pistols
on each hip. You couldn't tell
just what he thought of you. Had he hated
us, he wouldn't have shown it. When,
in that reasoning, mildly troubled tone
of his that meant he might
be disappointed in his son, he once explained,
In war, people hurt with tools,

I shuddered. You couldn't imagine what
he might invent. He was a patient man.

PROLEGOMENON

Up all night with a hundred dying chicks
in the jaundiced light of the coop,
my father steps into the first pools of day
pausing at the door to scrape the dung from his boots,
leaning his back to the jamb as he thumbs small
curls of tobacco into the burnt-out bowl of his pipe.

All night his ears rang between the echoes of his heart
with the sickly *cheep, cheep* of small white heads,
mouths agape from twisted necks, beaks drooped open
to ask what no one ever knows, refusing
feed and drink as they died,
twisted in the palm of his hand.

As the sun tears itself open on the blades
of new roofs where orchards he farmed once stood,
he strikes a match, draws deep, and the gray mare
ambles into dew from musky shadows in the barn,
dark tail switching the first flies of the day.
Squinting into the light, a pain too subtle to name

settles into his chest, and as he begins his chores,
morning spreads over him like a stain.

MY FATHER'S NECKTIES

Last night my color-blind chainsmoking father
who has been dead for fourteen years
stepped up out of a basement tie shop
downtown and did not recognize me.

The number he was wearing was as terrible
as any from my girlhood, a time of
ugly ties and acrimony: six or seven
blue lightning bolts outlined in yellow.

Although this was my home town it was tacky
and unfamiliar, it was Rabat or Gibraltar
Daddy smoking his habitual
square-in-the-mouth cigarette and coughing
ashes down the lightning jags. He was
my age exactly, it was wordless, a window
opening on an interior we both knew
where we had loved each other, keeping it quiet.

Why do I wait years and years to dream this outcome?
My brothers, in whose dreams he must as surely
turn up wearing rep ties or polka dots clumsily
knotted, do not speak of their encounters.

When we die, all four of us, in
whatever sequence, the designs
will fall off like face masks
and the rayon ravel from this hazy version
of a man who wore hard colors recklessly
and hit out in the foreign
bargain basements of his feelings.

ELEGY

My father was born with a spade in his hand and traded it
for a needle's eye to sit his days cross-legged on tables
till he could sit no more, then sold insurance, reading
the ten-cent-a-week lives like logarithms from
the Tables of Metropolitan to their prepaid tombstones.

Years of the little dimes twinkling on kitchen tables
at Mrs. Fauci's at Mrs. Locatelli's at Mrs. Cataldo's
(*Arrividerla, signora. A la settimana prossima. Mi saluta,*
la prego, il marito. Ciao, Anna. Bye-bye.)
—known as a Debit. And with his ten-year button

he opened a long dream like a piggy bank, spilling the dimes
like mountain water into the moss of himself, and bought
ten piney lots in Wilmington, Sunday by Sunday
he took the train to his woods and walked under the trees
to leave his print on his own land, a patron of seasons.

I have done nothing as perfect as my father's Sundays
on his useless lots. Gardens he dreamed from briar tangle
and the swampy back slope of his ridge rose over him
more flowering than Brazil. Maples transformed to figs,
and briar to blood-blue grapes in his look around

when he sat on a stone with his wine-jug and cheese beside him,
his collar and coat on a branch, his shirt open,
his derby back on his head like a standing turtle. A big
man he was. When he sang "Celeste Aïda" the woods
filled as if a breeze were swelling through them.

When he stopped, I thought I could hear the sound still moving.
—Well, I have lied. Not so much lied as dreamed it.
I was three when he died. It was someone else—my sister—
went with him under the trees. But if it was her
memory then, it became mine so long since

I will owe nothing on it, having dreamed it from all
the nights I was growing, the wet-pants man of the family.
I have done nothing as perfect as I have dreamed him
from old wives' tales and the running of my blood.
God knows what queer long darks I had no eyes for

followed his stairwell weeks to his Sunday breezeways.
But I will swear the world is not well made that rips
such gardens from the week. Or I should have walked
a saint's way to the cross and nail by nail
hymned out my blood to glory, for one good reason.

TOM CRAWFORD

MY FATHER THE INVENTOR

I.

In theory at least
it takes three geese to make a tree
flying out and back
the full length of their roots
finding water
even in the dark
or this poem
reaching all the way back to my father
who couldn't keep his hands off wood
"Inventing makes sense," he said
and he made two-legged chairs to prove it
and the love seat
the invention he liked best
the way it could separate
(if you wanted)
like our family
flying God knows where
a theory I can't let go of

II.

My father is much older now
but his eyes still shine
like that stainless steel
water driven
automatic potato peeler
he worked on twenty years ago
and through the glass he says,
"Tom, it's too complex to explain,
and I can't write about it
because the screws read everything,
but I've done it,
I've invented perpetual motion
and I've got it hidden in a box
up in Palmdale."
Now he's excited in the old way
and I tell him that's wonderful
and mean it
Later I walk back to the gate
escorted by a guard—
It is like this with my father
He is one hell of an inventor

DEAD ON HIS FEET IN LACKAWANNA

Like weather, your father's moods
were the world. And changed.
Some mornings
it would have been so easy
for him to slide in the Chevy & go—
Texas, California, who knows
what a man is capable of
without six kids.
                        But he stayed.
Thirty years, the scourge of Lackawanna,
he fed the drill press what it wanted.
Thirty years of working-class swagger,
wearing the sweat-oiled stink of a reliable
machine, wearing cigar smoke & khakis,
his balls on his sleeve, he could give
the old "fuck you" to the foreman
or a fist in the face to Mattie
the Mafia loan shark, & no one
would mess with him—till the day
his ring caught in the drill press,
making hamburger of one hand & mangling
half the other when he tried to pull it free.

Now, every time you see him
he's smaller. Soon he'll have shrunk
to the size of your son.
You could carry him in your lunch box.
You could hold him in the palm of your hand:
lift him to your mouth & tell him
you learned in your own good time
to make something human out of bitterness,
to call it a job & work it
like an old excuse. And when he asks
for a story, you tell him the one
he used to lull you to sleep with,
the kind of story it doesn't matter
whether you believe or not, you tell it
the way you heard it, a thousand years
before you were born . . .

    In a certain town lived a man.
    Every day he got up in the dark
    three hours earlier than he wanted to.
    He hoisted the morning on his back
    & went to work. He was always tired
    & his hands were always dirty.
    The earth was his enemy
    & swallowed him a day at a time.
    But he wouldn't go easy.

He'd drag the sky
down with him if he had to.
He was a man, dammit.
He had hands.
He brought home the bacon.

THE STORY OF LAVA

Every time I smell Lava soap it is 1948.
My father is bending over a long sink in the
pressroom of *The Sioux City Journal* at 5 A.M.,
his grey long-underwear peeled down over his
white belly, a thin bar of Lava tumbling over
and over slowly in his ink-stained hands.
The morning news has passed through his hands
out into the morning streets into the hands
of sleepy boys who fold it a certain way and
fling it on porches and steps, but that is not
my story. Lava is my story and the morning
news that Lava can't rub off. It is my father
bending over a sink, a thin bar of Lava tumbling
over and over and over slowly in his cloudy hands.

MY FATHER'S WARS

Once he followed simple rules
of casual strength,
summoned violence with the flick
of combat ribbon or hash mark;
now he forces a pulse into treasonous muscles
and commands soap opera villains.
He is camped in a world regimented
by glowing tubes,
his olive-black skin begging for the fire
of unlimited color.
In towns where he can follow
the orders of silence,
gunfights are replayed
in thirty-minute intervals
familiar as his stiff right arm
or the steel brace scaffolding his leg.

By midday the room is filled
with game shows and private eyes hurling
questions against all those who swear
their innocence;
his wife is in full retreat
and jumps when he answers in half-formed words

of single grunts deadly as shrapnel.
He need not remind her
he is always the hero;
the palms of his hands
are muddy with old battle lines.
He has fallen
heir to brutal days where he moves
battalions of enemies;
his mornings are shattered with harsh echoes
of their electronic voices.

Here he is on neutral ground
and need not struggle to capture words
he can no longer force his brain to master;
he plans his roster
and does not attend to his wife's
rapid-fire review of the neighbor's behavior.
He recalls too clearly the demarcation of blacks,
of Buffalo Soldier and 93rd Division.
By late afternoon he is seen rigidly
polishing his car in broad one-arm swipes,
its side windows and bumpers emblazoned
with stickers: US ARMY RETIRED REGULAR

ARTURO

I told everyone
your name was Arthur,
tried to turn you
into the imaginary father
in the three-piece suit
that I wanted instead of my own.
I changed my name to Marie,
hoping no one would notice
my face with its dark Italian eyes.

Arturo, I send you this message
from my younger self, that fool
who needed to deny the words
(Wop! Guinea! Greaseball!)
slung like curved spears,
the anguish of sandwiches
made from spinach and oil,
the roasted peppers on homemade bread,
the rice pies of Easter.

Today, I watch you,
clean as a cherub,
your ruddy face shining,

closed by your growing deafness
in a world where my words
cannot touch you.

At 80, you still worship
Roosevelt and JFK,
read the newspaper carefully,
know with a quick shrewdness
the details of revolutions and dictators,
the cause and effect of all wars,
no matter how small.
Only your legs betray you
as you limp from pillar to pillar,
yet your convictions remain
as strong now as they were at 20.
For the children, you carry chocolates
wrapped in goldfoil
and find for them always
your crooked grin and a $5 bill.

I smile when I think of you.
Listen, America,
this is my father, Arturo,
I am his daughter, Maria.
Do not call me Marie.

UNDER AN OAK IN CALIFORNIA

When Hitler kissed the children
and Mussolini played the violin
my father planted spindly cork oak
saplings in the dust of California
because they said this war might
never end. "The nation will need cork
and wood and shade," the foreman said.

He with a crew at an awkward march
over the hills above some snug town
with a saint's name took two steps,
swung his short hoe at the call dividing
earth, and one thin blade of life
from the bag at his belly rooted there,
then the crew lurched forward.

Maybe the rain would come, or maybe
the crew return with water packs.
"Plant many, for many will die," the foreman
said, while Hitler kissed the children
and Mussolini played the violin.

FOR MY FATHER

Sturdy English oak, deep-rooted
in the Wealden clay,
now ivy is slowing down your pacing
still in muddy fields
to sow, mend hedges, count cattle
or grow an oasis of vegetables and roses
in a wilderness of stinging nettles.
You take pride in your honesty
yet know that acorns are the food of pigs.
The brown eyes, observing England
for eighty-three years now,
have dimmed, yellowed like the leaves
in autumn.
Through two World Wars, when brothers
and nephews wore uniforms,
and bombs left smooth craters even
in the quiet Front Meadow,
you went on supplying milk and sugar beet.
But when an angry cow attacked,
you threw the toddling daughter down
beneath you in the ditch
and took the goring horn in your own back.

AT DAWN, SITTING IN MY FATHER'S HOUSE

I.

       I sit quietly
in the dawn; a small house in the Missouri breaks.
A coyote pads toward the timber, sleepless as I,
guilty and watchful. The birds are commenting on his
passing. Young Indian riders are here to take the old
man's gelding to be used as a pickup horse at the
community rodeo. I feel fine. The sun rises.

II.

       I see him
from the window; almost blind, he is on his hands and
knees gardening in the pale glow. A hawk, an early riser,
hoping for a careless rodent or blow snake, hangs in the wind-
current just behind the house; a signal the world is
right with itself.

       I see him
from the days no longer new chopping at the hard-packed

earth, mindless of the dismal rain. I hold the seeds
cupped in my hands.

III.

      The sunrise nearly finished
the old man's dog stays here waiting, waiting, whines
at the door, lonesome for the gentle man who lived here. I
get up and go outside and we take the small footpath to the
flat prairie above. We may pretend.

from INSIDE FRANCE: RETURN FOR MY FATHER

In cemeteries
They push carriages.
By the graves they
Sit,
Stroll,
Think.
I am here to see that.

I am here because the job I have
Is no longer there.
O job,
    You have been the amazing artichoke.
    Pulling back all your leaves,
    I never found your heart.
    I will get back to my occupation.

*

I am here for Normandy,
I am here for my father.

Onto the coast they fell,
Rushing the sleeping wood.
Onto the coast they came.
It was moonlight,
It was moonlight.

The beach
The cliffs
The underbrush.

Old place of great voyagers,
How did you lose Paris?
Were you at sea? Were we late?
We had to make flammable soldiers.
It takes flammable soldiers.
Were we late?

The beach
The cliffs
The underbrush.

I was a child asking,
"Father, Father,
Did you kill somebody there?
At the war, Father,
Did you kill somebody there?"

The beach
The cliffs
The underbrush.

Imhotep, father of medicine,
Be merciful unto us.

Soldiers without fear,
For your survival
Wear one gas mask,
Five grenades.

Soldiers without fear:
The farmer gave them wine.
Soldiers without fear:
The farmer danced
And gave them wine.
Soldiers without fear:
The farmer hid them,
In the barn he hid them,
He gave them wine.

But for the wine—
But for the wine—
It may not be this way again:
One gas mask,
Five grenades.

In a corner of my mind
It rains.
Were you wounded?
I have wondered.
For I have not healed my father.

ALZHEIMER'S

He stands at the door, a crazy old man
Back from the hospital, his mind rattling
Like the suitcase, swinging from his hand,
That contains shaving cream, a piggy bank,
A book he sometimes pretends to read,
His clothes. On the brick wall beside him
Roses and columbine slug it out for space, claw the mortar.
The sun is shining, as it does late in the afternoon
In England, after rain.
Sun hardens the house, reifies it,
Strikes the iron grillwork like a smithy
And sparks fly off, burning in the bushes—
The rosebushes—
While the white wood trim defines solidity in space.
This is his house. He remembers it as his,
Remembers the walkway he built between the front room
And the garage, the rhododendron he planted in back,
The car he used to drive. He remembers himself,
A younger man, in a tweed hat, a man who loved
Music. There is no time for that now. No time for music,
The peculiar screeching of strings, the luxurious
Fiddling with emotion.
Other things have become more urgent.

Other matters are now of greater import, have more
Consequence, must be attended to. The first
Thing he must do, now that he is home, is decide who
This woman is, this old, white-haired woman
Standing here in the doorway,
Welcoming him in.

MY FATHER'S LOVELETTERS

On Fridays he'd open a can of Jax
After coming home from the mill,
& ask me to write a letter to my mother
Who sent postcards of desert flowers
Taller than men. He would beg,
Promising to never beat her
Again. Somehow I was happy
She had gone, & sometimes wanted
To slip in a reminder, how Mary Lou
Williams's "Polka Dots & Moonbeams"
Never made the swelling go down.
His carpenter's apron always bulged
With old nails, a claw hammer
Looped at his side & extension cords
Coiled around his feet.
Words rolled from under the pressure
Of my ballpoint: Love,
Baby, Honey, Please.
We sat in the quiet brutality
Of voltage meters & pipe threaders,
Lost between sentences . . .
The gleam of a five-pound wedge
On the concrete floor

Pulled a sunset
Through the doorway of his toolshed.
I wondered if she laughed
& held them over a gas burner.
My father could only sign
His name, but he'd look at blueprints
& say how many bricks
Formed each wall. This man,
Who stole roses & hyacinth
For his yard, would stand there
With eyes closed & fists balled,
Laboring over a simple word, almost
Redeemed by what he tried to say.

F. D. REEVE

THE UNBEARABLE LIGHTNESS OF LOVE

Morning light pours
            from the whitewashed sky
like golden honey,
            perfuming the air;
by noon
       butterflies electrify the woods;
the scent of fresh-cut hay
            drifts everywhere.

Ungrateful sons
          push old men toward death
as if wealth and youth
            were complete success
like the rings around
         raccoons' tails
elevating them
       to episcopal eminence.

Imagine harmony instead,
           a choir of bells
across the lake
       and in the field the sons

mowing,

        their bare backs shining, signifying:

"Fathers,

          thanks for the field.

                    Your lives went well."

On the soft breath of early summer,

                  as the land

swells

      and the fiddlehead ferns uncurl,

                    I would sever

the pity

      from the war of the journey.

THOSE WINTER SUNDAYS

Sundays too my father got up early
and put his clothes on in the blueblack cold,
then with cracked hands that ached
from labor in the weekday weather made
banked fires blaze. No one ever thanked him.

I'd wake and hear the cold splintering, breaking.
When the rooms were warm, he'd call,
and slowly I would rise and dress,
fearing the chronic angers of that house,

Speaking indifferently to him,
who had driven out the cold
and polished my good shoes as well.
What did I know, what did I know
of love's austere and lonely offices?

PAUL ZIMMER

Intimations of Fatherhood, Operation Desert Rock, 1955

You trudge in shock across
the slain desert toward
the stem of the explosion
the appalling fungus sprinkles
spores down onto your helmet pot
onto the shoulders of young men
everything you see is dead or suffering

You were brought here
to be brave and mindless
but some small thing bumps against
your boot   a baby jackrabbit
blinded and matted with blood
you pick it up   feel it quiver twice
before it swoons in your hands

Without thinking   in midst
of this blasted place   you undo
a pocket and slip
the rabbit child into the warmth
then fasten the button again

70

you hurry to catch the others
walk on with them bearing
your secret toward the fire

FATHERS ARE NOT STONES

Fathers are not stones, though their voices
may be gravel, their lips granite-white,
nor are they stars set in the black night
to guide us—not stars, not distant suns,
though their light pales with age.

Father, if not stone, why is the path
to your heart so rocky, such a cold climb
to the top? if not star, why do you burn
in sunlight?

Stones are not fathers, nor are sons stars
to warm them when their wrists ache with cold
and their old hips break, when the heat rushes
out of them like a wing in flames.

If not star, a small fire, a saving ledge.
A handhold will heal me. If not stone,
then yield your softness. Father, warm me
so I have life to give.

JOINING THE STORY

The child's lateness was not yet resistance
to adult demands. He had merely forgotten
time and would be reminded by the hands
of his father who waited, so deep in his own story
of terror and loss that even the angry beating
of his heart was fear. When he saw the boy he joined

the ends of his belt in his hand and rushed to join
his child down the street before resistance
on either part. The child did not see the beating
coming, and if he saw it, he has since forgotten
his father's face then. The setting of his story
was lower: his father's legs, belt, whirling hands

between parked cars, his own warding hands
out of his picture of black curbs, sidewalk-joins,
one glimpse perhaps of a girl in the second storey—
people all over the night and no resistance
in the warm air to the sounds of what's been forgotten
long since, some talk, a radio, a quick beating—

minor, and nothing like the beatings
the father got. One of them at the hands

73

of a young soldier may not be soon forgotten
because he will tell his son, and it will join
those things that are passed on about resistance.
The father struck the soldier in the story.

The man kept spitting in his food. That story
happened in a labor camp, and the beating
was severe, with no chance for more resistance
in a room where they had sticks in their hands,
the first soldier and the others who joined in.
Not killing him, though—perhaps they had not forgotten

some small thing yet, in all they had forgotten.
Later, he'll want the father to recall the story
of his little beating though how can the son enjoin
him to? He cannot say on this date my beating
happened—you frightened your son with your hands
and your belt. He knows his father's resistance

to memory. His father has forgotten that beating
when his son, late, took the story from his hands,
joining it after the worst and without resistance.

FATHER HUNGER

Your father walks in the sun,
hands in pockets, eyes transfixed
on the ground as if the earth
were treacherous.

You tell him you need
to hear his voice. He
mumbles that he is short
of money for a new car.

You tell him you love
him. He says he is lonely,
that his shoes were too tight
when he was a child,

that blood soaked his socks
when he walked by the bully's
house on his way to school
under the dead trees.

You tell him about the opium
tea you drank alone

in the mountains at seventeen,
how you saw his thoughts

across the miles as breasts
hung from trees, the nipples
small bursts of light
like stars beckoning

just out of reach of his lips.
He says he is hungry, the day
frightfully warm. He says
his father was a silent man.

He says . . .

ELAINE LALLY

CHICAGO, 1938: AT THIRTEEN, FIRST GLIMPSE OF DADDY

I lean against the hot serge seat,
peer through a gritty train window,
clutch a snapshot.
He waits on the Illinois Central platform.
He looks like Gary Cooper
in a blue seersucker suit.
There are deep underarm stains
like wet half-moons.
He sucks long pulls on a cigarette.

The woman with him
gestures with forked fingers
of her right hand
that she wants a cigarette.
She is ignored.
Gary Cooper can't decide how to hold
the baby doll he carries, so he tucks
it under his arm, then lets it dangle
upside down by one leg.
The pink organdy dress
falls over the china face,

exposes stuffed muslin legs.
With his right shoe he grinds out
the cigarette, looks up toward
the train. He is not smiling.

THE PRESENCE OF ABSENCE

It was on a subway platform, waiting for an endless train
I said to him, "I need money."
(Did I say that?)
I had been coached into it.
At ten a mother coach can be ferocious on a field
when the football is the son
and the goal the returning of the father.
In that kind of game, kicking from any yard will do.

He was taking me home. We had spent three hours together.
I can't remember where we went, what we did.
I know we said little in sequence, or of consequence—
he might be respecting my silence, even then I thought.
Damn him for the convenience of his *noblesse oblige,*
but that I would not say nor ever have till now.

When he returned I liked him less for coming back.
I had loved his going, not for the rightness of it
but because I felt in awe of his foe—
now she was humbled, and I could take his place.
Such complexes become the building of our lives,
but a hole remains in the structure—
those years never lived never die.

When I see a father walking across a field
or sliding through a sand lot, or catching the fly of a stream
I cannot forget what is impossible for me to remember.

YOUR TRUE ISLAND

You were called José, Jerry, Horacio,
And on my tongue, each name still has its taste.

My mother, with her melted lipsticks,
Even in stories, she disguised you well:

You were a missionary from the Philippines,
A psychiatrist from Cuba.

Twice, you were honorable and hardworking—
Most often, a very cruel man.

When I watched packs of dogs
Or men carrying their girls from church

I imagined everything you could have given me
And everything I could have taken.

Whatever your true island
Whatever color your eyes

My firstborn son will carry it in his walk.
He will bear it in the glance his eyes cast.

I cannot hang my black clothes
On the idea of you.

Or mark a page in my prayer book
For the wish of you,

But tonight, father, the dreams of you
Seep into my pillow
Like strings of honey in a hot tea.

MY PARENTS

I'm falling asleep again without my parents' arms
around me. Because I'm no longer their child,
I ask a quarter of the people I meet
to put their arms around me. Some say no
and walk away; others become like a blanket
thrown off in fever.
These are complaints!

My accusation is (if I could I'd say it
in a way to bring them to their knees):
When I'm cold, I'm afraid.
When I'm warm, I'm afraid.

After my son's first nightmare
he climbed into my bed—
I teach this child and myself:
we hold each other tight so we won't die.

MARIAH

I conjure with your name, pronounced like *messiah*.
Tell me, what do you know about our father?
Did you know he was a drinker, a brawler, a poet?
It took my mother a while to figure out he wasn't just

a man's man. Of course, he died young.
You must know that.
Poetry is a dangerous thing
but it's gentler on the liver.

Did he ever, whiskey-wet under the arms,
lunge at your mother with a knife?
And when he was with your mother
how many others were there?

I know for instance your mother is French
and that you are an only child.
My mother later married a man named France
who gave me his name. Whose do you have?

There's a painting I want to show you.

"The Two Fridas" sit holding hands, their open
hearts joined by one artery. Staggered twins:
diastole and systole. No room around or roof
over them, just a background of storm-cloud sky.

Mariah, there may be many more of us.
I know of one other, older than we, a boy,
born to a woman, probably only a girl,
in rural South Carolina. One of the few times

I saw our father, he told me about this half brother,
sad that the boy, his son, didn't even know about him
the little I know, and I suppose you know.
His mother didn't want our father "coming around."

Do you remember his eyes? Crème de menthe and milk.

Our half brother's world sounded so moonshine
and shotguns. Knowing nothing of country life
I imagined him—Li'l Abner, and his mother
smoking a pipe, popping out of a ragged midriff.

You know it wasn't guns
your mother and he ran in Spain.
I read in a biography of a famous writer,
another man's man and his sometimes friend,

about the time our father got caught
smuggling marijuana from Mexico
with "Pops," his scrawny, tattooed father and
a pregnant, sunburned girl, looking "like a tomato."

Whose mother is she?

My mother says yours married
a pilot afterwards, and that you lived
for a time in Ethiopia. I've lived in Africa, too.
Once above you and once below.

When he was in prison, did your mother send him
photos of you? Not long ago I read for the first time
his letters from Leavenworth. He cajoled, he cursed,
he spat ink but got nothing from mine.

Mariah, your name is everything unknown
that I must know.
I hope you are as you sound:
myrrh, myth, miracles.

If you read this, come to Mexico.

I will greet you with *mariachis* and marigolds.
We'll go to the Museum to see "The Two Fridas"
and together we'll build one memory.
Please, Mariah, I'm missing so many stones.

An Early Mystery

Six years old,
I'm lingering over the candy counter.
On the other side of the bodega
my mother is interrogating the grocer
about the freshness of the produce:
the breadfruit, the yuccas, the plantains.
She does not trust him, I can tell.
I recognize the voice she uses
from listening late at night
when my father's late arrival
makes her sound that way: like a radio
picking up a faint signal,
then losing it.
               Sometimes,
he comes in to kiss me, while I pretend
to sleep; but there are nights
when I hear the door click shut again.

Though involved in my task
of deciding over chocolate-covered coconut bars
that I can make last, or the bubble gum
wrapped in tiny English-language comic strips
that he can translate for me later,

I smell the woman approaching: familiar scent
of gardenias, cinnamon, alcohol—
my daddy's shirt and his breath
when he leans over my bed.
                              She stares at me
as in a trance, kneels down to look into my eyes.
Embarrassed, I hang my head, notice a run
racing up her stockinged knee toward her plump thigh
like a little jet on a tan sky, until it vanishes
under her tight black dress.

Are you his little girl?

                              Suddenly,
Mother is between us, pulling me away
before I can answer, or make my choice
of sweets.

I hear her walking toward the street, high heels
firing back at us like cap guns. On the aisle
where Mother and I stand holding hands,
there is something in the air so strong—
we could have followed it with closed eyes
all the way home.

A COLLAR ROUNDS MY THOUGHT

Priest, my father, priest,
your collar cuts my neck,
my resonating breath's
intake
at knowing you were naked,
the collar jettisoned,
a crescent on the floor
where the bed upheld
my mother's pity for your sex.
Your strict lips kissed
her thirty years of fear,
kissed them away,
her dainty bones
under your own
barely moving
like the quarter moon
lighting the room,
like the tightening collar
caught in the light
choking desire
in the penitent hours
before my birth.
Priest, my father, priest,

your collar rounds my thought
like a moon, refractory and white.

Latin scholar, library dust
on your face, glossing tomes
next to her breath.
Only intellect
before her flesh
set your loins on edge.
Then transfixed,
desiring her
as the lame desire miracles.
Two scholars at dusk.
Not Héloïse nor Abélard,
neither their youth
nor calamitous love.
Priest, my father, priest,
your collar rounds my world
like an equator
burning to know your life
interred forever in that faith
which primed your guilt.
No stigma on the grave,
only your name witnessed by rain
and I, your bastard child.

A Spin

I.

Who remembers running boards,
the way a man could stand, one foot perched,
peer down the blouse of his neighbor's wife—
how her hand touched his naked arm,
as she leaned out

or the way girls sat on the running boards
of their fathers' cars,
trading secrets before he left for work
and shooed them off to school?

Tiptoe, I stood on the running board
of my father's Packard for a kiss.
"I'll be back soon," he called,
driving off with a woman
beside him, "and take you for a spin."

In the late afternoon, I dozed at my post.
Miles away, the windshield splintered,
the radio stopped like a heart.
Saying good-bye is all I remember of him.

II.

Each year my father grows dimmer,
our home movie romance, cut, shelved, over,
leaving hardly a glimmer.

My sad childhood self would whimper,
saying adieu to him, my leading man, that rover.
Each year my father grows dimmer.

A gambler, my Rhett Butler, a wooer
of women, his daredevil act left me lonelier,
leaving hardly a glimmer

of the man he was. But I forgive his disappearing one summer.
Thank God that hurt is over.
Each year my father grows dimmer.

After a lifetime letting go of the simmering
love-hate duet with my first heart-throbber,
leaving hardly a glimmering

of the perfect parent in my second-grade primer,
now I have found a real lover.
Each year my father grows dimmer,
leaving me hardly a glimmer.

THE LOST PILOT

for my father, 1922–1944

Your face did not rot
like the others—the co-pilot,
for example, I saw him

yesterday. His face is corn-
mush: his wife and daughter,
the poor ignorant people, stare

as if he will compose soon.
He was more wronged than Job.
But your face did not rot

like the others—it grew dark,
and hard like ebony;
the features progressed in their

distinction. If I could cajole
you to come back for an evening,
down from your compulsive

orbiting, I would touch you,
read your face as Dallas,
your hoodlum gunner, now,

93

with the blistered eyes, reads
his braille editions. I would
touch your face as a disinterested

scholar touches an original page.
However frightening, I would
discover you, and I would not

turn you in; I would not make
you face your wife, or Dallas,
or the co-pilot, Jim. You

could return to your crazy
orbiting, and I would not try
to fully understand what

it means to you. All I know
is this: when I see you,
as I have seen you at least

once every year of my life,
spin across the wilds of the sky
like a tiny, African god,

I feel dead. I feel as if I were
the residue of a stranger's life,
that I should pursue you.

My head cocked toward the sky,
I cannot get off the ground,
and, you, passing over again,

fast, perfect, and unwilling
to tell me that you are doing
well, or that it was mistake

that placed you in that world,
and me in this; or that misfortune
placed these worlds in us.

ORPHANS

When my father died, leaving me
distraught for never having known
him as father, as friend,
for never having known myself

as child of one whose eyes and mouth
and temperament were mine, my mother
cautioned me, told me not to mourn
what I perceived as loss:

you and I are daughters of the wind,
she said, you and I are fathers
of our souls, sprouting intact
like seedlings from two wind-borne

acorns. We thrive on luck, she said,
there is no father's love in that.

from BOTTLES

*

One winter, somewhere in the Whiteface Inn
on Whiteface Mountain, no phone, nowhere to run,
where the bottle was delivering a talk
at a Potato Chip Convention, he got me
alone in our complimentary cabin,
lit a fire, fanned it with vodka,
and began the night-long assault
on my mother and her evil stepmother
who'd smile and stab me in the back when my head was turned. . . .
No, the first time was years before, in Miami,
in a restaurant where the red booths were crowned
with bronze and leather horses' heads,
he said the thing about my grandmother being a witch;
afterwards, I was afraid to sleep in the same room with her
though I don't remember believing anything he said. . . .

*

The liquid in these bottles was always colorless.
I think I believed it was neutral,

like the stream of hotels and motels
I occupied in his custody.

I always gave him the latest Gillette
for whatever the holiday.
(In those days the razor improved every year:
Edges for every beard.

Mandelstam wrote that though this blade cut
like sedge grass, bent but didn't break in the hand,
it was the product of a dead trust . . .
the shareholders—"packs of American and Swedish wolves. . . .")

And once, in Cherry Hill, when he started in
on my mother and her family again
I grabbed his Gillette out of his dopp kit
and held it to his throat.

OEDIPUS REFORMED

I will not kill my father,
he must die of admiration.
I will not lay a hand on him,
I will not curse or nag
or make him to explode angrily
so that his mind bursts.
Here is myself realized,
I have everything I ever dreamt,
and I shall attend his funeral,
mourning my lost heart;
for with him goes my impulse.
And then I will raise him in my eyes,
we will be one.
My wife will play my mother
and be kind.

THE FATHER

Now it seems that he has done wrong and
all of mankind quickly conspires to convict him as unfit,
a monster. But what has happened?
>   Hasn't he touched the thing he loves with love?

Now he thinks he will lock himself in a closet and eat darkness.
He will be the cockroach that scurries across white porcelain.
Nothing again will ever near him that is pure,
>   not a toy or a photograph or a thing with wonder . . .

It was only that he was reaching
as if to hand her a compliment and had fondled her breast
when all he'd wanted was to fondle her heart
>   but it was his daughter hidden there inside and now everything
>   is in disorder.

Now he will be a shadow falling through formless years and
one touch will touch him again and again
and find him crumpled with awe in someone else's flesh
>   watching two hands that cannot be trusted.

BILLY UNDERWOOD: MEMORIAL DAY

Uncle gives his Chevy horn three sharp toots.
Mother bangs shut her new reincarnation book
and puts on rubber boots and Father's black raincoat.
The moment has come. There's no way out.

I slump in the back seat and say nothing,
a temporarily benched home run slugger
rubbing spit into the pocket of a catcher's glove.

The car starts and we're off to the graveyard.
Mother clutches two American flags from the dime store
to plant at the foot of Father's headstone.
Uncle drives slowly, tries to stay calm.

Father is only a fading memory these days,
a crabby guy who could throw a neat knuckle ball.
When I dropped a toss his scorn burned like fire.

Mother wouldn't let Father out of her sight.
Father put up with Mother as long as he could,
then left home to join the Air Corps again.
He crashed in West Berlin. Mother never cried at all.

Uncle pushes the flags into the spongy earth.
Mother raps on Father's carved stone and says,
"You won't get away with this, Howard. I won't let you."

A big grackle flies across the wet pine trees.
Mother's eyes look awful funny, real spooky.
"Let's get out of here," I say to Uncle.
"Mother is hating Father more than ever now."

ROWING

Early Saturdays
father and I argued to the lake,
oars strapped in a V
to the Chrysler.

He insisted I feather them,
roll my wrists so the oars
cut air with least resistance,
enter water without sound.
No good. My left arm weak
I pulled in circles.
We shifted seats and he rowed
ruler-straight.

Because we spoke by shouting
I tasted my hands' blood
on a college crew
snowy Aprils
as the coach stood silent
and huge in furs,
superior as a yacht
as we slid and grunted past.

One summer
I drove father to the lake
bitter from old failures
and rowed—contemptuous, nervous—
oars skipping despite my skill.
It was an invitation to conversation,
the stiff locks squeaking
"I love   I love."

THRALL

The room is sparsely furnished:
A chair, a table and a father.

He sits in the chair by the window.
There are books on the table.
The time is always just past lunch.

You tiptoe past as he eats his apple
And reads. He looks up, angry.
He has heard your asthmatic breathing.

He will read for years without looking up
Until your childhood is over:

Smells, untidiness and boring questions;
Blood, from the first skinned knees
To the first stained thighs;
The foolish tears of adolescent love.

One day he looks up, pleased
At the finished product.
Now he is ready to love you!

So he coaxes you in the voice reserved
For reading Keats. You agree to everything.

Drilled in silence and duty,
You will give him no cause for reproach.
He will boast of you to strangers.

When the afternoon is older
Shadows in a smaller room
Fall on the bed, the books, the father.

You read aloud to him
"La Belle Dame sans Merci."
You feed him his medicine.
You tell him you love him.

You wait for his eyes to close at last
So you may write this poem.

DAUGHTERS AND OTHERS

Zelda Fitzgerald began to see
people as ants and felt afraid.
Lucia Joyce said scornfully
"They buried father, but he's not dead.
He's watching us all."

Shishkebab of paternal heart
Sylvia gladly would have eaten.
Skewered flesh, rejected blood,
of such stuff those songs were written.

Sylvia's died when she was eight.
How could it be enough to hate?
Love's appetite is unappeased
and I was seventeen.

Daddy, Daddy, shaped in fingers,
nestled unbecomingly
in grumbles, glooms, impatiences,
somehow a blurred blueprint lingers.

Blessing or curse of what might then have been,
the point is what is unsubtractable.

They buried father, but he's not dead.
He's watching us all.

You clever ladies, dead and mad,
fathered and husbanded by fame
(was that it?) that you never had,
scorched by an incandescent name,

or flailing at what put you here
to suffer and create like them,
you stayed as naughty as the cute
precocious girls you all had been,

lavishly smeared them with the gay
sulfurous colors of your wit,
Indian givers, pretty bitches.
And your eyes were all alike:

bright, moist, vulnerable,
always untrusting, slewing back
for some approval from the wings.
You have it now, you know:

biographies swelled fat
on each premenstrual peeve
will make you pinup martyrs
for future women's movements—

not an inconsonant fate.
Smash that father!
Scrunch that hubby's smug skull
with the frying pan you cook his breakfast in!
Uproot, abolish, triumph.

What stern, indulgent wraith will be on hand
to scold and slap and kiss you afterwards?
They buried father, but he's not dead.
He's watching us all.

MEN AT FORTY

Men at forty
Learn to close softly
The doors to rooms they will not be
Coming back to.

At rest on a stair landing,
They feel it moving
Beneath them now like the deck of a ship,
Though the swell is gentle.

And deep in mirrors
They rediscover
The face of the boy as he practices tying
His father's tie there in secret,

And the face of that father,
Still warm with the mystery of lather.
They are more fathers than sons themselves now.
Something is filling them, something

That is like the twilight sound
Of the crickets, immense,
Filling the woods at the foot of the slope
Behind their mortgaged houses.

WILL INMAN

MY FATHER IN HURRIED FLASHES

in spring and summer, he rose early. trousers,
shirtless, only filmy BVDs over his pale chest.
spoke with chickens and pigeons as he fed them.
the breed dog shadowed him, eyes turned up, adoring.
the man noticed tomatoes and okra blooming, corn
stalking straight and tall, no tassel yet,
pole beans curved vines around the stalks. he
cocked his ear at a mockingbird in the pear trees.
a black and gold garden spider wrote lightning
letters down a wide web atop the grape vines,
white and purple scuppernongs.
                              my father hummed
to himself in the garden. or whistled. Mrs C,
next door, said it was to make folks think he
was happy. but Dad had sung tenor in two quartets,
one spiritual—they'd sung at five hundred
funerals; the other, The Rat Poison Quartet, for
laughs.
        he married for appearances, i imagine,
but his mother held on with barbwire tongue. my
mother's soul was scored to marrow by the ancient
methodist.
          the man had vision. he laid roads all

111

through swamp country in eastern North Carolina,
arched two bridges over islanding rivers.

                                        he
could sell hinges off the gates of hell. he never
learned to say *Negro*. he hated snakes. when i
began to bring the creatures home, he knew i was
devil possessed. he taught me wild plants, where
to look for Venus flytraps, and to keep an eye
open skywards for shooting stars.

                        his God had a
fetish for sin and carried threats of fire. we
were much alike but believed differently: he died
grieving for my sins. i live, mulling his.

MICHAEL S. WEAVER

MY FATHER'S GEOGRAPHY

I was parading the Côte d'Azur,
hopping the short trains from Nice to Cannes,
following the maze of streets in Monte Carlo
to the hill that overlooks the ville.
A woman fed me pâté in the afternoon,
calling from her stall to offer me more.
At breakfast I talked in French with an old man
about what he loved about America—the Kennedys.

On the beaches I walked and watched
topless women sunbathe and swim,
loving both home and being so far from it.

At a phone looking to Africa over the Mediterranean,
I called my father, and, missing me, he said,
"You almost home boy. Go on cross that sea!"

MNEMONIC

I was tired. So I lay down.
My lids grew heavy. So I slept.
Slender memory, stay with me.

I was cold once. So my father took off his blue sweater.
He wrapped me in it, and I never gave it back.
It is the sweater he wore to America,
this one, which I've grown into, whose sleeves are too long,
whose elbows have thinned, who outlives its rightful owner.
Flamboyant blue in daylight, poor blue by daylight,
it is black in the folds.

A serious man who devised complex systems of numbers and rhymes
to aid him in remembering, a man who forgot nothing, my father
would be ashamed of me.
Not because I'm forgetful,
but because there is no order
to my memory, a heap
of details, uncatalogued, illogical.
For instance:
God was lonely. So he made me.
My father loved me. So he spanked me.
It hurt him to do so. He did it daily.

The earth is flat. Those who fall off don't return.
The earth is round. All things reveal themselves to men only
   gradually.

I won't last. Memory is sweet.
Even when it's painful, memory is sweet.

Once, I was cold. So my father took off his blue sweater.

THE RACE

This dream is green
And actual memory:
My father and I
In the neighbor's yard,

Having just stepped
Forth from the woods,
In summer, evening,
The light gone gauzy

About the shrubbery.
Perhaps it is joy
In the strangeness
Of our being together

Alone in such a place,
Or maybe it's only
The way the lawn slopes
Down its long expanse

Into our own backyard
That makes me dare him
To the race, first
One home the winner.

And am halfway there
And certain when he
Simply passes me by,
His trousers a thresh

Of fabric flowing
Smoothly on my right,
And then the amazing
Sight of him running

Steadily beyond me,
This father of chairs
And silences, halt
Figure of my youth.

How could I know then
My pursuit of him
Would never again come
Gladly to such an end?

STEPFATHER

Twenty years, and it's his face I see,
the one I loathed beyond mere turning
from the world we had to occupy,
beyond indifference. Now my real old man,
who left for reasons no child could understand,
all agreed upon and legal and remote,
was easy enough on weekends, a few summer weeks,
a big chum with a billfold and a gift
for making a kid feel temporarily
safe: but on the ordinary weekdays,
when mornings came down bone cold,
or on summer's last dog days
when the air stood still,
with this stepfather it was nip and tuck,
an awful game of stare and snarl,
acting out new-fangled Greek tragedy
of urgent hatred with a man
who began as stranger
and became my closest enemy.

In his presence my blood shifted
currents, and when I smiled coolly
to pass him off, at his slightest glance,

I flinched, darkened, steeled my eyes,
and couldn't help but take in every word.
Yet when I think of my own father,
his grin is just a blur, his features fade
what he must have said is lost,
but of this step-in father I recall
every wrinkle, line, and mole
on a face that stared so calm
the sky could crack and the sun fall through,
and the worst was the salt of his asides,
his few tossed words that stirred my anger
toward cold wisdom, not forgiveness,
but toward a vow I would never forget.
And slowly my coiled hatred unwound.

Nowadays we're known to speak
quietly at family get-togethers,
to share a wry word or two—
though don't think we're friends,
exactly, the kind who slap each other
on the back or howl at some past incident:
we keep our distance, step lightly
at the outskirts of our limits,
like two brothers, one elder, with his eye out,
the younger, leery, watching from the wings.
Though people say there's something in our eyes
that matches, catches fire the same:
and when they meet, I know we restrike

some old bargain we made years before
after we came to understand each other
beyond our fears and hatred,
beyond simple father-son.

BLANK PAPER

Blank sheets of paper were my inheritance.
A plain envelope below my uncle's face,
my dead father's life in legal miniature:
the paper nowhere mentioned my name. Erased,

vanishing as the ink had vanished,
I crept from the couch where I slept, TV
still on to morning cartoons, just outlines
of people, as I was, blank inside. To be

was to be denied. I nearly laid my head
on the open oven door, but it was messy
with meat juice and baked-on drips of sauces
I had made when alive. I held me,

rocking my outline below the TV,
where I watched the cartoons from the floor as
I had as a little girl, my father
blacked out on the couch. Now blank paper has

the life I tried to restore there, after
feeling I was nothing. The feeling, too,

is my inheritance, but the true gift
is to re-create all the old anew:

My head on an oven door just repeated
the way I was disinherited. For him to give
me my life long ago was what I needed,
thus what I write both re-blankens my life
and fills it in with a right to live.

BRIEFCASES

Fifteen years ago I found my father's
    in the family attic, so used
        the shoemaker had to
repair it, and I kept it like love

until it couldn't be kept anymore.
    Then my father-in-law died
        and I got his, almost
identical, just the wrong initials

embossed in gold. It's forty years old,
    falling apart, soon
        there'll be nothing
that smells of father-love and that difficulty

of living with fathers, but I'd prefer
    a paper bag to those
        new briefcases
made for men living fast-forward

or those attaché cases that match
    your raincoat and spring open
        like a salute
and a click of heels. I'm going

to put an ad in the paper, "Wanted:
　　　Old briefcase, accordion style,"
　　　　　and I won't care
whose father it belonged to

if it's brown and the divider keeps
　　　things on their proper side.
　　　　　Like an adoption
it's sure to feel natural before long—

a son without a father, but with this
　　　one briefcase carrying
　　　　　a replica
comfortably into the future,

something for an empty hand, sentimental
　　　the way keeping is
　　　　　sentimental, for *keep-*
sake, with clarity and without tears.

Variations on a Theme

When my daddy sang barbershop
in the shower the steam flushed
out under the bathroom door
to jolly the air with notes so
sweet   the weather vane swung
south   the saxifrage oozed
down in the swamp. My daddy was
a four-part sea chantey   water
sizzled a coy castrato to his tenor
while pipes pumped up a buffo.
The copper walls throbbed a cool bass.

When I sing barbershop in the bath
my voice is so shaky I can
only luck my way through
a bubbly blues. If a quarrelsome
chord knocks me under I can
probably rise on the next crescendo
but I'll never be like Daddy
in the shower   he could translate the catbird into a cat
with a warble from the windpipe
cozy up the dog with the dove.

While Mom sits quiet by the stove
poor thing   tone deaf.
And mute   since Daddy left.

A Picture of My Father

Going through boxes after my mother's death, I come across a little packet of photos of a bare-chested young man who has photographed himself in a full-length mirror. Understand I am upstairs in my own new house, a man in early middle age, rich in worries, with dust rising around me from the previous generation. *Dust to dust* we say at funerals. It's something young men do, taking pictures of themselves in mirrors. I know he is my father because I have looked as hard into mirrors as he is looking, a little radio in the corner playing the popular music of the day—crucial—light flaring from the mirror, making a kind of nimbus. I can recognize Narcissus, after all, when I see him. There is always music & light & the naked human body. There is always the battle against delight. There is always marriage, in which we yearn toward an impossible lyric grace. All fathers are the wrong father.

SHAVINGS

The monk's head
Gleamed like polished wood,
Dead a good while.
"Who were the Sadducees," I asked.
Sad, sheepish smile,
The old shepherd with his bad ear cupped,
Nodding: "They didn't believe in the resurrection."
I might have been an axe addressing an obdurate stump

When the phone broke me from sleep,
Something inside
Coming loose like a stamp in water,
Floating on the surface,
Alone, able to look back down,
The cool walls of the glass
Like the eyes of that old monk,
A pair of question marks.

To see with quiet clarity
Old age, the self reduced to a question,
A stub of lead pencil
Using itself up,
The years curled like shavings around it.

A Black Soldier Remembers:

My Saigon Daughter I saw only once,
standing in the dusty square across
from the Brink BOQ/PX, in back of
the National Assembly, not far from the
ugly statue of the crouching marines facing
the fish pond the VC blew up during Tet.

The amputee beggars watch us.
The girl and I have the same color
and the same eyes.
She does not offer me one of
the silly hats she offers Americans
but I'm not Senegalese and
I have nothing she needs but
the sad smile she already has.

ANTHONY PETROSKY

MY FATHER'S VOICE

When he talks suicide,
I tell him there are reasons to live,
and he tells me, with that voice,
that I don't know what I'm talking about,
that I don't know the pain he feels.
He says it with the voice now inside of me,
the one that speaks and snaps out
when I am afraid or angry,
and I have begun to hear it in my sons.

This is the voice that says it has had enough,
it will do what it wants,
stay away, listen, be warned,
maybe to protect itself,
to conceal the pain,
or maybe it's only power or rage
that wants to go on living,
a survivor, misplaced
from the Depression or war,
trying to pass itself along,
trying to find a place in my sons.

DRAGGING THE LAKE

Father I keep dragging
my lake for you, near sleep
I row through dark bogs
where logs soften
and fan into fungus,
and vanish overnight.

Sometimes I see the pale,
bloated skin of your absence,
translucent down to the clean
fingernails.

Sometimes your belly
rolls in a green lake
and I glimpse the swollen,
stretched suture-marks
that score you down the middle
from when they tried to fix
your clogged heart.

I'm searching for the part
of you that anchored in
to the deepest me—the hush

within your thin
gasp of pipesmoke.
So many glowing words,
sucked into ash.

MY FATHER CANNOT DRAW A MAN

On the paper he shoves across the desk
sprawl three figures, three attempts
—two, really. One slopes off
to the left, sprouting a bowler
from its funhouse head. Beside it
squirms an eyeless chameleon
with two tails. The last is a hard
wavy line.
       The doctor studies them,
jots some notes beneath, clears
his throat. Trauma, he explains,
can make the brain lose track
of the place the body occupies,
of the borders and crosswalks between
where you are and where you're not
till every street leads back
to the same vacant lot. Many
can adjust, he says, but you must watch
such patients. They can wander off,
step out to get the mail and disappear
with hardly a trace.
       My father and I
watch a man rise from the paper

and wander off toward evening traffic,
outline unsteady, sloping left,
no shoes, baggy slacks, his hat
too large. Lights flow up the street
before him. My mother stands
at a crosswalk down the block,
where the light blinks, *"wait, wait."*
When he steps off the curb, cars
glide through him. He takes on
their colors, or they take his on.
Hurrying into the rush, he leaves
a hard wavy line.

SUCH COUNSELS

My father would always come
back from the barn
as if he had been in conference.
He had farm in him the way
some men have pain.
Every night the feed, the one
thing to get him home straight.

Still, he was a one-armed man,
toting his bottle
like a book of hours.
And he could sleep standing.
Each year to kill those cattle
he had to drink a week in a day
to stay cold sober.

DAVID WOJAHN

HEAVEN FOR RAILROAD MEN

You're still a young man,
he says, not to his son,
it's his bitterness he's
talking to and
at the restaurant
he orders a fourth round
before dinner.
With Mother wiping
her glasses at the table,

I help him from his chair
to the john. He pees slowly,
fingers like hams
on his fly, a complex
test of logic
for a man this drunk.
I'm splashing cold water in his face

and he tells me he's dying,
Don't say a thing to your Mother,
and please, Dave,
don't ever remember me like this.

I remember how you said you
needed to ride
the baggage cars forever,
passing prairie towns
where silos squat like
pepper shakers on dry earth.
I want to be six again
and sway with you
down the sagging rails
to Minot, Winnipeg, and beyond,
your mailsacks piled
like foothills of the Rockies.

You're unloading your government Colt,
unzipping your suitcase
for Canadian inspectors.
Father, when I touched you
I was trembling.

Heaven for railroad men
begins with a collapsed trestle.
The engine goes steaming
off into nothing.
There are no rails to hold you.
You're singing country-western
at the top of your lungs.
You go flying forever,

the door pulled open,
mailsacks scattered
into space like seed.

PETER MARKUS

My Father's Wrench

The metal feels cold
in my hands
like I'm shaking
my father's hand.

My father's hands
were big-knuckled
bastards, callused,
dirt and grease
beneath the nails.

I grip the wrench,
look for a loose
nut that needs
tightening, something
that won't be hard
to fix.

THE DESK

My father is chopping up the desk he built me when I was a kid to get smart leaning over looking at books he bought me so I could get out of town and be better than him, and not have to work for a living like he does, but sit around on my fat ass week after week, developing longer and longer arms so I can pat myself on the back, or reach all the way across country and pinch him now and then, just to see if he's still alive, which is getting him pissed off.

PHYLLIS BECKER

WHERE YOU COME FROM

He spotted me at my table,
Walked over from the bar
To talk to me, to tell me
About myself, he said, but
Talked about his son in
Cambridge, Harvard '78
Graduate. His big brown
Hands were holding a Scotch
On the rocks, eyes coming
Into focus, words tumbling
Over themselves. He asked me
How I got there, told me how hard
He worked, how his son got to
Harvard, how he went to Howard,
How he was going to tell me about
Myself, but talked about visiting
His son and how his feet got tired
Walking on cobblestone, and his son
Taking him to his nice apartment
When all he wanted to do was
Find a bar and listen to
Some slow jazz, and not to get
Him wrong, he loved his son,

The "arrogant son of a bitch,"
And how, if I ever saw a shoe
Shine man, to respect him, or
A waiter, busboy, porter, and
Didn't I know to remember where
I came from, and said with a shrug,
How he was here, and his son
Was there as if that said it all—
And something about blue lines
And red lines and all those
Lines that separate one from
Their own, and as I got caught
Up in his words, he reminded me
Of my old man after a few,
Who I learned to never listen to,
And as I listened to this man
Talk his way from this bar
To his days at Howard University
Yard to cobblestone in Cambridge
To a son he sacrificed to a world
He thought he understood, I wondered
If some man or woman in some bar
Across town was sitting
With my old man trying to find
Where they came from.

THE LOST AND LAST HAYRIDE NORTH

for Hank Williams (1923–1953)

I'm driving Hank Williams to next gig
up north, lost on Highway 61, and he's
drunk in the back seat telling me how
queer it feels to be a daddy, lots of
money coming in. My own? He left us,
Mr. Williams, ran clear to Cincinnati.

Pontiac running blind in a snowstorm,
he's broken out his guitar, mumbling
lyrics about a log train coming home,
his pa limping up to the porch, gone
off again to a cypress cutters' camp.
That's one dandy picture of your boy,

I mention to him, watching my mirror.
A spike in spine, he grins, the pain's
dead and, yes, you already said he's
a junior I reply. No children of my
own right now I guess is sad but how
much further tonight in my new hearse?

WHEATFIELD

You disappear into its rowless height
to where the sun is best, somewhere
beyond the middle. I can't see you
select a head, hold it between your thumb
and finger, wrench it from its long stalk.
I can't. I'm a small girl bored in the car
that sits in a dusty ditch. It's too hot
for meadowlarks. There's only the oil drip
to tattoo out the hours. You taste the kernels.
They're sweet, almost juicy. The whiskers
of chaff stick out from your ruminant face.
You'll spit soon. I become breasted
in the wait, the radio's on, clouds
polka dot the wheat's rhythmic shimmer.

Once I see your greying head over a patch
of rye. I assume you're busy pulling it up,
as it's wild and out of place. I'm
in the front seat now, kneading a man's
shoulder to compare it with yours. Has
he baled hay? I'll examine his chest.
When the grain rolls without any wind,
I suspect your approach, but it's only

a mouse running from a weasel. At times,
the two tails of the road curl in the heat
and come together. It's never sunset.

The car doors open and close like the wings
of a preening fly. I guess you're not lost,
except to me. Only my plow-shaped jaw
and my tendency to strong thighs call up
your fatherly presence. That is, until
my own son stands at the field's edge,
his arms akimbo and his feet firm
as two shoots, and he wants to know
if the wheat's ripe yet.

NUDE FATHER IN A LAKE

I've never stopped, even in my sleep,
seeing him in the lake
facing me with his hands all wax
over his sex.   His throat
and his wrists are burned.
He is so white.
He splashes me with water.

I yank my baggy swim trunks off,
dive, and reach cold mud.
I hold a submerged branch.
His nudity no longer shimmers . . .
a dance . . . a fish . . . green cartilage
between his eyes . . . a hinged mouth.

I surface and watch dad
retrieve his clothes from a bush.
He keeps on walking without asking
me, entices me to follow, from the rear.

CERTAIN PEOPLE

My father lives by the ocean
and drinks his morning coffee
in the full sun on his deck,
speaking to anyone
who walks by on the beach.
Afternoons he works
part-time at the golf course,
sailing the fairways like a sea captain
in a white golf cart.
My father must talk
to a hundred people a day,
yet we haven't spoken in weeks.
As I grow older, we hardly talk at all.
I wonder,
if I were a tourist on the beach
or a golfer lost in the woods
meeting him for the first time,
how his hand would feel in mine
as we introduced ourselves,
what we'd say to each other,
if we'd speak or if we'd *talk*,
and if, as sometimes happens
with certain people, I'd feel,

147

when I looked him in the eye,
I'd known him all my life.

LONG DISTANCE HOME

In your album tattooed
with Army Air Corps patches,
the women in tinted photos
were dark and naked

and wore their hair frizzed
wild as a wolf pup's fur.
They held amazed piglets
to their breasts which stretched

tubular to their waists,
astounding our eyes and tongues
that formed their nicknames:
Fuzzy Wuzzies.

Slouched in a wrinkled uniform,
you stared from pictures, Father,
framed by jungle, centered
in your cocky smile.

In others, you sprawled
like a child at play behind the machine gun,
your wire-rimmed glasses
mirroring vine light. You

told us you were forgotten
on New Guinea for two years
and made gold jewelry to forget
the jungle rot in your knee,

the man who committed suicide
in your tent, the way your spine
cramped around guns in tails
of B-25s during battles

we had to memorize in school.
Later in North Africa and Italy
you grew so tired of destruction's
crazy names, you cried

as you pounded the floor of your plane:
Sweat and Pray.
Now, half a continent away,
your voice hollows, recalling

the lonesome frenzy of birds
lifting paradisical wings
over a strafed jungle at dusk.
In my kitchen on Discovery Bay,

across remembered halftones of light
I hear your laughter warm as whiskey.

THOSE THINGS

Preparing to talk to my son, I remember
my father in the hospital bed, slowly
becoming tangled and lost among a maze
of tubes, and when from a chair by

the window I asked if there was anything
he regretted, he answered, "I'd go to
church and I'd have talked to you about
those things." With long strokes

that bent my body like an oarsman,
I massaged his swollen calves.
We had never touched except
to shake hands, and only once

did I cry to his face, when I accused
him of not caring, when I was
young and cared, but in those last
months, when flowers lined

the window sills and I read
to him, we held hands. I never
saw him naked, and I haven't
seen my son naked in years,

though I know his body is being
driven to collide with others.
Yesterday on the basketball court,
when he raised his arms to shoot,

I saw dark tangles of hair.
I wonder what more it was
my father had wanted to tell me
that one evening just after I had

learned to drive, and he walked
over to the Volkswagen. I started
the engine, and he leaned toward
the window, as if to whisper.

Though no one was near, his hand
covered the side mirror when he said,
"Protect yourself." That was it
and I backed out of the driveway.

JOB THE FATHER

I have made my bed in darkness.
—Job 17:13

all his children in the same house
and a great wind comes
out of the wilderness

seven sons three daughters
all his eggs in one basket
and a great wind comes

reading the story I am paper
curling to avoid the flame

and no matter what I ask them
the stars say *yes yes yes*
all over the sky

I have but one son all my children
in one place always

and I am still here Lord
in the desert where even my fear
has grown a little courage of its own

saying *take me Lord*
take only me
and I will forgive you everything

from LATE LIGHT

*

In June of 1975 I wakened
one late afternoon in Amsterdam
in a dim corner of a library.
I had fallen asleep over a book
and was roused by a young girl
whose hand lay on my hand.
I turned my head up and stared
into her brown eyes, deep
and gleaming. She was crying.
For a second I was confused
and started to speak, to offer
some comfort or aid, but I
kept still, for she was crying
for me, for the knowledge
that I had wakened to a life
in which loss was final.
I closed my eyes a moment.
When I opened them she'd gone,
the place was dark. I went
out into the golden sunlight;
the cobbled streets gleamed

as after rain, the street cafes
crowded and alive. Not
far off the great bell
of the Westerkirk tolled
in the early evening. I thought
of my oldest son, who years
before had sailed from here
into an unknown life in Sweden,
a life which failed, of how
he'd gone alone to Copenhagen,
Bremen, where he'd loaded trains,
Hamburg, Munich, and finally
—sick and weary—he'd returned
to us. He slept in a corner
of the living room for days,
and woke gaunt and quiet,
still only seventeen, his face
in its own shadows. I thought
of my father on the run
from an older war, and wondered
had he passed through Amsterdam,
had he stood, as I did now,
gazing up at the pale sky,
distant and opaque, for the sign
that never comes. Had he drifted
in the same winds of doubt
and change to another continent,
another life, a family, some

years of peace, an early death.
I walked on by myself for miles
and still the light hung on
as though the day would
never end. The gray canals
darkened slowly, the sky
above the high, narrow houses
deepened into blue, and one
by one the stars began
their singular voyages.

WHAT IF I DIDN'T DIE
OUTSIDE SAIGON

So what do you want? he growled inside the chopper,
strapping me roughly to the stretcher
as if I were already dead. "Jesus," I swore,
delirious with pain, touching the hot mush of my legs.
"To see my wife. Go home, play with my kids,

help them grow up. You know." His camouflaged face
was granite, a colonel or sergeant who'd seen it all.
He wore a parka in the rain, a stubby stale cigar
bit tight between his teeth, a nicked machete
like a scythe strapped to his back. He raised a fist

and held the chopper. He wore a gold wrist watch
with a bold sweep-second hand. The pilot glanced back,
stared, and looked away. Bored, the old man asked,
Then what? his cigar bobbing. I swallowed morphine
and choked, "More time. To think, plant trees,

teach my kids to fish and catch a ball."
Yeah? he said, sucking the cigar, thinner
than he seemed at first. Through a torrent of rain,

I saw the jungle closing over me like night.
"And travel," I said, desperate, "to see the world.

That's it, safe trips with loved ones. Long years
to do whatever. Make something of my life. Make love,
not war." I couldn't believe it, wisecracking clichés,
about to die. He didn't smile, but nodded. *So?*
What then? "What then? Listen, that's enough,

isn't that enough?" His cigar puffed
into flame, he sucked and blew four perfect rings
which floated through the door and suddenly
dissolved. Without a word, he leaned and touched
my bloody stumps, unbuckled the stretcher straps

and tore the *Killed-in-Action* tag from my chest.
And I sat up today in bed, stiff-legged, out of breath,
an old man with a room of pictures of children
who've moved away, and a woman a little like my wife
but twice her age, still sleeping in my bed.

WORDS FOR MY DAUGHTER
FROM THE ASYLUM

Alas, that earth's mere measure strains our blood
And makes more airy still this parentage.
The bond is all pretending, and you sleep
When my affections leap
And gasp at old hope vainly in my night's cage.

Dear marvelous alien snippet, yes, you move
Like a down-raining cloud in my mind, a bird
Askim on low planes under lightning thought,
An alter-image caught
In gossamer seed, my most elusive word.

There must be some connection, more than mood,
The yearning wit of loneliness, and more
Than meets the law on that certificate.
Strangers do not create
Alliances so deep and dark and sore.

Yet we are strangers. I remember you
When you began, a subtle soft machine;
And you remember me, no, not at all,

160

Or maybe you recall
A vacancy where someone once was seen.

I can address you only in my mind
Or, what's the same, in this untouching poem.
We are the faceless persons who exist
Airily, as a gist
Of love to twist the staid old loves of home.

Strangers we are, a father and a daughter,
This Hayden and this Martha. And this song,
Which turns so dark when I had meant it light,
Speaks not at all of right
And not at all, since they are dim, of wrong.

Distance that leaves me powerless to know you
Preserves you from my love, my hurt. You fare
Far from this room hidden in the cold north;
Nothing of me goes forth
To father you, lost daughter, but a prayer.

That some small wisdom always may endure
Amidst your weariness; that lovers may
Be kind to you; that beauty may arouse
You; that the crazy house
May never, never be your home: I pray.

THE FATHER

The father's entire body
is heavy tonight. This father, like all other fathers,
feels lost sometimes. Finding the way back home seems
all too impossible.

I don't remember getting lost.

I clearly remember the infant spark. The brilliance
of my disbelief. I also remember the hours strung
together like a necklace of voices. The days, months,
lifetimes even whizzing by as the automobile splashes
through the street.

Nearby an elm bristles with rain & the
ocean carries the change in our pockets & the plump
hours of our afternoons in its tremendous body. Our
hair feels swept & our bones feel as though they are
made of darkness.

At three years old a face
can shape joy & very quietly absorb neglect into its
shadowy blue eyes. The father drinks every infinitesimal
ounce of the joy & carries every elephant of sadness
inside his stomach.

Fathers, as sure as I am here today, you
fathers of paperweights & fathers of forged tools.
Fathers of white flour on your elbows & fathers of
daily intimidation. All you fathers that sail on ships
& on the thirst for freedom. I say again, I simply
don't remember getting lost.

As Seen at the Uffizi

An audience of shepherds
Looks on adoringly
As Mary gently bounces
The babe upon her knee.

To Mary's side stands Joseph.
He isn't looking on.
His gaze is middle distance.
He wishes he were gone

Up into the high mountains
That rim the little town
To dwell among the shepherds
Till things have settled down.

LINDA PASTAN

BETWEEN GENERATIONS

I left my father in a wicker basket
on other people's doorsteps.
Now I wait to be adopted by children,
wait in a house far between generations
with night rising faster
than the moon.

I dream of Regan laughing on her father's lap
behind the castle.
I laughed once in my father's face,
and he laughed, and the two laughters
locked like bumpers
that still rust away between us.

My children fill the house with departures.
Zippers close, trunks close, wire hangers jump
on the empty pole—ghosts without their sheets.
And I ask what strict gravity
pushes love down the steep incline
from father to child, always down?

My Daughter As a Nuisance

It breaks my heart
That's how my aunt
Or uncle would
Have said it. I
See her circle
The burdock pile
The dog snapping
At her ribbons.
She stumbles, cries.
All is fever
In the noon sun
In the pitiless
Growing up that
Left me running
In weeds toward my
Father a long
Time ago and he
Turning as if in
Ordinary petulance.
Does that sacred fence
Still stand? I followed
Too close at heel
Into the clearing

Where for once
Bending with hoes
We were united
Hill family
Poorer than poor
With no Kodak
To record our heart-
Break and the strange
Fare of love and the
Lack of love as we stooped
For greens or to destroy
Ourselves in the hills
Where the weeds walled
Us in till we grew tall,
And broke in the sun.

SPEAKING

I take him outside
under the trees,
have him stand on the ground.
We listen to the crickets,
cicadas, million years old sound.
Ants come by us.
I tell them,
"This is he, my son.
This boy is looking at you.
I am speaking for him."

The crickets, cicadas,
the ants, the millions of years
are watching us,
hearing us.
My son murmurs infant words,
speaking, small laughter
bubbles from him.
Tree leaves tremble.
They listen to this boy
speaking for me.

To My Daughter

How will you know
how much I love you?
you who are now

an unopened leaf in a bud this cold March
I had thought the word "father"
meant failure, inadequacy, loss

until a friend reminded me
how "father"
applied to me too

then the word went through revolution
as all goes through revolution
inside time

know that I become real
as you do.

RON McFARLAND

TELLING THE FUTURE

In this photograph all my children
have noses,
            even the bewildered baby,
my button-nosed son.
Seeing his sisters
            I know he'll
grow out of it,
            establishing the family nose
like a business.
            My father had a nose
for business, but he never sniffed
the sweet perfume
            of success.
Left that to me, he said once,
and the grandchildren.
            He loved to sneeze
terribly from his good Scottish nose
during slow days
            when pollen
hung in the humid air
like grudging customers
            slow
with their dollars.

170

My daughters
will marry good, small-nosed men
whose fortunes are nothing to sneeze at.
Everyone says my son
looks like his mother.

SAUL'S PROGRESS

1

I told my son:
"Stop trying to screw the monkey's tail
Into his bellybutton.
Originality
Is never its own
Justification.
Some innovations
Get nowhere."

"The Sunday monkeys are my friends,"
He said.
I was on my way down
From the heavenly city
Of the 18th-century philosophers.
He was on his way up,
Almost three.

2

"Moby Dick is smarter than
The other dicks."
A song to make the
Bad guys happy.

You sang it all day Saturday
With snot-filled nose
And clouded eye,
To raise me
To a fury.

3

You sit on the crest of a dune
Facing the sea,
Which is beyond sight.
Your anger at me
Makes you play by yourself,
Tell stories to yourself,
Fling out your hurt
To the wide sky's healing.
A red boat in one hand,
A blue in the other,
You begin singing songs
About the weather.
Cliff swallow, brilliant skimmer.

4

As if he were me, he comes bounding in,
All happiness. I owe him
All happiness. For these years at least.
When he smiles and says, a good time,
I have no notion who else
He has made happy with my happiness.

173

from PLIGHT

I. THE SEAL

My father
early rose
gone before
my waking

Into his
footstep of
snow I now
set my own.

II. THE TALK

My son says to me:
"Why must we die?"
I am looking out

over the river
as it passes
into the mountains

and my eyes go out
beyond the edge:
"That sky we call sky

there: there's our body."
He looks at me
trying to see it

and says: "Why must I
die?" In the stream
reflections of trees

are also rooted.
I want to point,
but see that I can't.

ANCESTRY AS REALITY

for Tarik

it was a friend saying
"look man, divorce
doesn't make bad children,
bad parents do," that stuck
in the weak side of better judgment.
so i pushed against the cycle—poor, black,
    fatherless—
to see if it would break.
it haunts me
with apparitions of my own father
his eyes beady as a pair of craps,
a bottle of cheap gin
on his kitchen table,
him, way off in Omaha.

when the measles, the whooping coughs,
father's day get you, when at school
the skilled surgeons cut the good black stuff
from your head, I may not be there.
but you'll have the weekends, summers,
me pleading—"Tarik, daddy loves you,
do you love daddy?" weekends

when i rub you 'gainst my hairless chest
& try to convince you
i wanted to be a man.

ROBERT STEWART

THE JOB LEFT TO DO

No matter what from now on
my son will not know his father
hugging and loving his mother.

Tonight in the dark, I turn
to a woman my son has never met

and I think of the job left to do:
Like this, my boy, hold her
a long time in your arms.

from NORTH PERCY

*

Playing too happily
on the slippery mountainside
my only son fell down and died.
I taught him to talk honestly
and without stalling come across
but I could not teach him the cowardice
and ambiguity
to live a longer life unhappily.

You see, girl, you ought not to
center your affections so,
little short of idolatry.
A young man is untrustworthy.
In the morning satisfied
he gets up from your bed
and in the evening he is dead.

*

His mother and I did our best, Lord,
for Matt, and it was pretty good,

and he for twenty years gave us
    the chance, without our disappointment or remorse.

But now this leaves us nothing
to blame or regret—only this bawling
    and the bright image that
    around the grave his friends confabulate.

*

THAT OTHER MAN AND I

He as wandering he walks
    up the hill to the mailbox
imagines, his mind lapsing,
    that my son is living.
We are among the steeplebush, I do not dare
    reach to him there,
bereaved are touchy. But I intend
    to leave him there behind
with his botany and try what it's like
    on a longer hike.

That man would rather go on
    mourning than his son be gone
for good. This is impractical
    even in dull
Stratford Hollow. I'll go roaming

among the screaming
cars in the city, carefully
        threading my way.
Let him go crazy
        back there without me.

A day will come when I am dying
        that we two again
may meet. And when we look like strangers
        into each other's
sullen eyes, what shall I say
        and he to me?
when once for all we join
        in absolute bawling,
blinding tears that blot
        the world out?

*

CHICAGO 1968

My son would have voted for the President
this year his first time, being twenty-one,
if he were not in jail or a refugee
in Canada, and if he were not dead
like the Republic: we are seeing scenes
reminiscent of Caligula.
How shall honest men respond to it?

181

Matthew would have known to tell me.
I was a champion of the resisting young.
I usually vainly tried to guide them,
more often guided. But my liaison
is lost. Now they are right to call me senile.

*

I doubt, though it is possible,
that when I die will be so bad
and I may yet go mad,
which they say is horrible;
but probably the worst that can befall
is past me now Matty being dead.

If he were here he would have hoed
this field where my shoulders fail,
except that he would be in jail
which he and we would cope with as we could.
He was a quiet one but stood
conspicuous and did not quail.

It is one year—I wish that August 8th
were blotted from the diary—
by now he glitters like a wraith
of mist on the mountain at midday,
and my sadness is joining with
the other sadness of humanity.

The Bones of My Father

1

There are no dry bones
here in this valley. The skull
of my father grins
at the Mississippi moon
from the bottom
of the Tallahatchie,
the bones of my father
are buried in the mud
of these creeks and brooks that twist
and flow their secrets to the sea
but the wind sings to me
here the sun speaks to me
of the dry bones of my father.

2

There are no dry bones
in the northern valleys, in the Harlem alleys
young / black / men with knees bent
nod on the stoops of the tenements

and dream
of the dry bones of my father.

And young white longhairs who flee
their homes, and bend their minds
and sing their songs of brotherhood
and no more wars are searching for
my father's bones.

3

There are no dry bones here.
We hide from the sun.
No more do we take the long straight strides.
Our steps have been shaped by the cages
that kept us. We glide sideways
like crabs across the sand.
We perch on green lilies, we search
beneath white rocks . . .
THERE ARE NO DRY BONES HERE

The skull of my father
grins at the Mississippi moon
from the bottom
of the Tallahatchie.

THE BOOK OF THE DEAD

—for H.R.

In Egypt, they wrote
on anything—

on the inside of coffins, of eyelids,
on the inside

of their own skin.
They sent their dead on a river of words,

to an afterlife
where everyone dwelled—

the innocent,
and the guilty,

and those who were both.
They took their bodies with them,

and their shadows followed them like children.
Father, you were a bitter man,

but there was grace
in the way you lapsed

like memory at the end—
like something

forgotten,
something

forgiven. This is my solace—
it is not the body

from which we are released.
It is the soul

which is lifted from us like a burden.

from POEM (FOR MY FATHER)

*

You should have married me off at sixteen;
or if I was too ugly then
at twenty in the hope that time
would improve me: or if not then
at twenty-eight to an old Marwari who needed heirs.
I had hoped to read to you
but my words are impaled in the silence
and only the centipedes moving
among the brown rotting flowers
hear the scream and are heedless.

In the first flowering of grief,
I believed in rebirth.
The second time the loam dries
and the scales fall from my eyes
I swear
to serve the sick and hungry,
to toil the land,
to pray to Jesus
and if I marry
to marry of my own people
and never go to America

187

or if I do, to throw myself
like a burning page
into her rivers of oil.
Certainly I will forget
all this foolishness of poetry.

I remain where I am.
In the dark sleep of August
your bones take root and seek
my house and I in my half
sleep, with one ear to the ground
hear the endless, soft hum.

*

Hearing of my arrival the squatters
wait burdened with melons and potatoes
at the edge of the forest.
I climb out of the jeep and go to them.
They see I am wearing trousers
and my hair is in a scarf.
They encircle me and salute me as your son.
The women wail and fall upon my neck
with their children, wide-eyed and shy
clinging to their legs.
Shamed already by their gifts
I do not tell them
I am only a girl.

Outside the circle an old man
with a stick in his hands
murmurs to himself,

The great man's son is always great
even when he is small
and the poor man's son is always small
even when he is great.

I see the circle tightens.
Beyond it is the jungle without roads
and soon it will be dark.
In the whites of a child's eyes
there are strong thin red ropes.

from FATHER DREAM

i

I still dream about his
failure. We are so poor
we must live in the park.
Someone has betrayed him
again. It's always cloudy,
the trees bare, their leaves
rusted shavings over the grass.
Each night we sleep on tombs
stained lime with mold, pull up
the quilts my mother weaves
from the spidery stuffing
of Spanish moss. I keep
saying to him it's
O.K., we're still alive. We're
all alive: it's so clear to me.
Yet he goes on, and we lie on tombs
under moss, listening as he wanders
all night, his voice
dwindling among the trees
as he drinks and weeps
the way he never would.

ii

"Adieu, adieu! remember me."—King Hamlet

You're taking me on a tour, the
landscape of your life, joking
about the greatest scenes:
the place you got caught
in a storm, "Here's where
the wind blows when it rains."
Of the willow pond where you
fished, "Here's where the ducks
have feet, though you can't
see them." At the house where
you were born you say
"There. That's where ghosts
swing from a clothesline all night."

TERMINAL

My father is coming home on this train.
Its headlight shatters the October rain
as it rocks across a narrow trestle
onto the island and blasts its whistle.
The dripping engine curves toward the station
with a hiss spread before it like a stain.

The past is no longer his dark domain.
I wander among the ghostly people
    my father is coming home
with, hoping he will know me with this cane
in my hand, know I have chosen the same
gnarled wood as his own two canes, light hazel
from southern Italy, with the curved handle
worn smooth. I can see him through the cracked pane.
    My father is coming home.

LARRY RUBIN

THE DRUGGIST

I. THE DRUGGIST

He came to me last night, as if there had never
Been a box. Routine, no tales of Hell
To tell, he worked on an old prescription, and I
Watched, as I used to when I was a boy, and stifled
My eyes, and from the corner of his eye
He saw me and asked why. But all that dirt,
I said, how did you get up
Past all that dirt? I
Can pull pegs out with my teeth,
He said, and went on working.
Later, just before the third cock crowed,
He handed me the jar. Son, he said,
I want you to deliver this before
You go. Is that all, I said, mustn't I
Avenge your death so you can rest? Just
Deliver that medicine, he said, and it was dawn
And of course he was gone. And I knew
That being sealed up like that had turned his wits
Because I saw he had made the label out
To me.

II. THE RUNAWAY

The night he died, they sent me out for candles
And that is when I heard the music sound
Where stars rode at anchor; everywhere
I heard that muffled band playing naval
Music, and saw him, cocky at sixteen,
Hoist his gear against his neck and stalk
Up the gangplank to see the world.
The stars danced, and he had girls, and I
Wasn't even born; but now above
The neon and the lights the sky is filled
With ships and my father struts with a sailor's gait.
All night I hear the music through the candles,
And watch the ships move slowly past the stars.

FOR A MILLINER

1

My father lives dying
Slowly in a metal bed.

He wants to be working,
Wants to bend over his table

Or turn to his machine,
Deft fingers sewing together

One last high fashion hat
For a proper Bostonienne.

2

Ten years of paralysis
Have forced his hands

Into his mind—there's nothing
To *do* there. So the horses

Of his childhood snort, ramp,
Rear, break harnesses,

Race flailingly off down
The unpaved streets, and prance

At the seaside, scattering
Sand, green girls, mothers,

And small children fresh
From sepia tintypes.

3

He dies weeping, his mind
strewn with pins, feathers

And felt, a band of leather,
And the horses running

Like a sewing machine
That can't be stopped.

In Ecstasy of Surrender

My father steps out
Into the vanishing point.
He dwindles. He is tiny.
He can't help himself.
It takes me a long time
To find him again.
I need a sharp pencil,
And then, all of a sudden,
I need an eyelash
To point with.

There where the lines draw close,
So alike, so severe,
I've never seen anything like it!
Him almost gone,
Emptying away.
A kind of groping it was,
Yes, a groping
While remaining stockstill,

And me, of course,
Wanting to follow
After him,

While being unwilling to
Just then.

SENTIMENTAL

The light has traveled unthinkable thousands of miles to be
condensed, recharged, and poured off the white white pages
of an open Bible the country parson holds in front of this couple
in a field, in July, in the sap and the flyswirl of July
in upper Wisconsin, where their vows buzz in a ring in the air
like the flies, and are as sweet as the sap, in these rich and ritual
    minutes.
Is it sentimental? Oops. And out of that Bible the light continues
to rush as if from a faucet. There will be a piecrust cooling
out of its own few x'ed-out cuts. And will it make us run
for the picklier taste of irony rolled around protectively on our
    tongues
like a grab of Greek olives? My students and I discuss this
slippery phenomenon. Does "context" matter? Does
"earned" count? If a balled-up fidget of snakes
in the underbrush dies in a freeze is it sentimental? No,
yes, maybe. What if a litter of cocker spaniels? What
if we called them "puppydogs" in the same poem in that same hard,
hammering winter? When my father was buried,
the gray snow in the cemetery was sheet tin. If I said
that? Yes, no, what does "tone" or "history" do
to the Hollywood hack violinists who patiently wait to play
the taut nerves of the closest human body until from that

lush cue alone, the eyes swell moistly, and the griefs
we warehouse daily take advantage of this thinning
of our systems, then the first sloppy gushes begin . . .
Is that "wrong"? Did I tell you the breaths
of the gravediggers puffed out like factorysmoke
as they bent and straightened, bent and straightened,
mechanically? Are wise old (toothless) Black blues singers
sentimental?—"gran'ma"? "country cookin'"? But
they have their validity, don't they, yes? their
sweat-in-the-creases, picking up the lighting
in a fine-lined mesh of what it means to have gone through time
alive a little bit on this planet. Hands shoot up . . . opinions . . .
questions . . . What if the sun wept? the moon? Why, in the face
of those open faces, are we so squeamish? Call out
the crippled girl and her only friend the up-for-sale foal,
and let her tootle her woeful pennywhistle musics.
What if some chichi streetwise junkass from the demimonde
gave forth with the story of orphans forced through howling storm
to the workhouse, letting it swing between the icy-blue
quotation marks of cynicism—*then?* What if
I wept? What if I simply put the page down,
rocked my head in my own folded elbows, forgot
the rest of it all, and wept? What if I stepped into
the light of that page, a burnished and uncompromising
light, and walked back up to his stone a final time,
just that, no drama, and it was so cold,
and the air was so brittle, metal buckled
out song like a band saw, and there, from inside me,

where they'd been lost in shame and sophistry
all these years now, every last one of my childhood's
heartwormed puppydogs found its natural voice.

My Father at Eighty-Five

His large ears
Hear everything.
A hermit wakes
And sleeps in a hut
Underneath
His gaunt cheeks.
His eyes blue, alert,
Disappointed,
And suspicious,
Complain I
Do not bring him
The same sort of
Jokes the nurses
Do. He is a bird
Waiting to be fed,—
Mostly beak—an eagle
Or a vulture, or
The Pharaoh's servant
Just before death.
My arm on the bedrail
Rests there, relaxed,
With new love. All
I know of the Troubadours

I bring to this bed.
I do not want
Or need to be shamed
By him any longer.
The general of shame
Has discharged
Him, and left him
In this small provincial
Egyptian town.
If I do not wish
To shame him, then
Why not love him?
His long hands,
Large, veined,
Capable, can still
Retain hold of what
He wanted. But
Is that what he
Desired? Some
Powerful engine
Of desire goes on
Turning inside his body.
He never phrased
What he desired,
And I am
His son.

from COLLECTED POEMS

*

Anchored here
in the rise and sink
    of life—
           middle years' nights
he sat

beside his shoes
rocking his chair
    Roped not 'looped
        in the loop
of her hair'

*

The death of my poor father
leaves debts
and two small houses.

To settle this estate
a thousand fees arise—
I enrich the law.

Before my own death is certified,
recorded, final judgment
judged

taxes taxed
I shall own a book
of old Chinese poems

and binoculars
to probe the river
trees.

*

I walked
on New Year's Day

beside the trees
my father now gone planted

evenly following
the road

Each spoke:
Peace

from THE UNCHRONICLED DEATH
OF YOUR HOLY FATHER

For the record: there is no record
of your father's death. He died
of a disease that is today
                    preventable.
In the land where you were
born, the current century has not
arrived—not so much as one damn gangrene
foot in the goddamn door—and so

> *If your old man were alive today,*
> *He'd live the same. He'd die the same.*

Since there is no record, I have elected
myself as chronicler. I have inherited
the unhappy task of representing
your father's death. It falls to me
to pick a name for your disease—
it will not do to remain in the country
of vague generalities. (In my chosen vocation,
lying is permissible—indeed encouraged—

but the lies must be specific.)
Cholera perhaps? Yes,

Cholera will do—it's in the news again.
A common fate? Why not? He was a common man.

THE ESPLANADE

I.

The ocean churns onto the old slabs
And old iron, as my father and I clamber
Over the esplanade in our jogging sneakers.
A hurricane shattered it when I was a boy,
But now the broken slabs, the color of bread,
And the prongs of wrenched iron, like crawlers
Weeping rust onto the eroded pavement,
Are a zone of permanent ruin along the water's edge.
Weeds thrust from cracks and scratch our legs.
My father's almost eighty years
Have cured him to lean, silent stiffness.

For years he worked nights, and slept all day
In a stale room at the other end of the house,
His head wedged under the pillows.

I imagine him clutching some gift
Along the tenement streets, when he was a boy,
Working at his father's laundry.
He preserved it in his mind,
A timeless falling world where he still lives;

The gift was for me:
An amazed distance only acrobats could leap.

II.

I spent summers here as a boy,
Peering out at the Rockaways,
At the white scooting chips of sailboats.
The bay was windswept, sparkling;
Its emptiness was half inside me.
I lay on a tilted slab, a radio jammed by my ear,
Listening to the love songs of those years:
Heartaches and night sweats were my music then,
As if my mind were a shell where something
Had drunk deep. It was the first of many rooms,
A blur of enclosure: a bedroom rank with adolescent sex,
Another room over Paris rooftops,
A bronze lamp, a clock with a twisted hour hand;
The innocuous matter of days
That took an impression, like soft wax.

This morning we follow the esplanade,
Full of awkward silence, athletic, lean,
Already preparing to jog into the next world.
My father talks in prepared sentences,
Always rehearsing about these waters he has walked
Along every morning for fifty years.
In his constricted voice, almost inaudible,

An exhalation from some crevice in his mind,
He talks about the devil, God's partner
In the human heart. These waves, he says,
May be heaven's heartbeat, but the blood
In our veins is the devil's work.
I too know the devil's work, which brings
Us together here, partners in movement, in failure,
As if he carried me even now in his lean body,
His mind grown sleepy from peering into a dimness.

III.

At the far end of the jumbled rock
And cement walk is a chain fence
And a bleak lawn, some unused benches;
The sort of building everyone knows,
A bland skin of squares and angles,
A nest of antennae, empty repeating windows.
As we skirt the fence, my father
Stares at the wintry expanse
Of ocean, grass, the building of tan brick,
With its small orderly windows.
It is a nursing home; my father is an old man.

Sea gulls waddle on the breakwater
Stabbing at bread rinds, or lift off
With powerful thrusts, to skim the incoming waves.
It is a bitter gift: that crashing line of white water,

The meeting of two realms.
My father and I share it now,
Both of us peer into the dimness.
All my life, I have wanted to come closer
To this mild, unforgiving man,
Who exists in my hands and voice,
And is the nervous laughter I hear
Before my throat expels it.

IV.

I remember my grandfather's quavering voice,
Sitting beside a window, a few days before he died.
He chanted in Yiddish to his grandson,
Who understood nothing, but stored everything in his memory,
Distended by unsayable fatigue.

An unpainted house, wind singing in the cracks,
The window casting a sheen on the long-unused sofa,
The bed with its sad quilt. On the table,
The photograph of a boy with large ears,
A crushed smile, standing beside his father,
Who squints beyond the camera,
A stiff, muscular, beautiful man.

V.

Father, there's so much I never asked you,
Now the answers seem trivial.
Yet, for all your angry quiet, your shy nervous body,
What have you saved by living less?

I think of your swallowed angers,
The hurt on your face when I twisted grammar.
All your life, you have wrestled with fears
That would not become angels.
Your crabbed masculinity concealed a motherly
Sweetness you could let out only when you were alone,
With the damp sand at your feet, the foaming waves
Beside you. With an artistry I still marvel at,
You remade yourself in that lonely space,
As you have remade yourself in me.

CROSSING COCYTUS

i

Arc of fire across the black of heaven: a father's fist
in downswing so that even the sun must avert its gaze. Midriff,
the muscles taut, rib on rib defined, the glint of honed mahogany.

A partial image trying to announce itself, so that one
is forced back on that and that alone as it blips across the mind.
To begin there, then, the shock at last acknowledged, and then

to let the meaning circle out, cold eccentric pulses from a probe
approaching an erratic world, the imagination refusing consolations,
wary of swerving to left or right. As with Jacob, seeing no way

out, confronting the stranger there before him, arms up
like a wrestler's, whose stance is meant to taunt and keep one's hips
off balance. Pinions creaking even yet, those pterodactyl wings

like windmill blades as they fan the long-dead air back into
motion. To circle without seeming to move, then to lunge, as now
your eye catches those taut claws circle into view, thumbs bent in

along the dirtcaked palms to keep from breaking when they strike,
the muscled neck, black as that corpse once glimpsed at carnival,
organ music piped into the psychedelic coffin, what had been

a woman once, dredged up from Salt Lake's depths, hawk's claws
going for your eyes, as now you face those twin fangs and then
those glowering half-mad eyes, and you smash back at last

against him in a frenzy of release in this agony of song, horn
hard, your right fist arcing down and over, as once he showed you,
that one shot shattering (noseridge, cheekbone, eye) the glass.

ii

The horn: held in different posturings. Ramshorn, trumpet,
tuba, sax, and horn of plenty. Aloft or swerving on its a-
symmetric line of force. Horn of ibex, horn of goat. In the crotch

of the arm, like so, or lifted to the disfigured lips
to sound a way-down note, fingers on the valves, as breath strains
to hold it there as a sign of inspiration. Sounds then the self

makes in its isolation: grunt, eructation, parrot squawk,
the mindless trumpet of the rectum become a point of force.
Breath: that universal given, sustained by some unseen Lover

even here along Cocytus. A thought to irritate the arid eye.
The bugle at the Chinese soldier's lips along the frozen Yalu
so that we froze in terror, tried in vain to warm our hands enough

to pull our cranky rifles from our blankets and waited for the shadows
to appear, howling in the predawn wind across that void. The rabbi
there at Belsen: Yom Kippur '44, cupping his shaking hands

to call the lost, his thin cry interrupted by the incoming train
with its fresh arrivals. Bull's horn, thick and dripping between
those thighs, brooking no refusal. The song of Cyclops repeating

the same crude strain. The highrumped gladiator lifting high
his horn, crowing the force of his contending, throwing down
his glove to anyone who dared oppose him. And yet. And yet I too

have been given and can give. Abba: daddy. My son, eleven, playing
scales up and down his trumpet, the sweet notes rising and falling
with the breath we gave him, she and I, thus shattering the glass.

iii
For weeks haunted by a sheen of purple marble, the gossamer
curtains rustling against the night's black jade. Not that
image on the refectory wall as at Padua, Pan as cartoon presence,

goat's head with wolf's fangs, draco, demon, not that but something
else: light gathering to itself, like a dying fire in the woods,
when one starts from some troubled sleep at three. Refusing

to reveal itself more fully, yet still fixed on the mind's eye.
Jacob, with the first hint of dawn, the cold light, after struggling
through the drugged hours with that shadow, feels the wind

shift and charges the heart be kinder to itself. And sees
the light grow then less alien. As on that morning, in the first
light of the March dawn, when we walked in groups or singly,

though we were none of us alone, and the road revealed itself
ascending, we heard the yellow grosbeaks and the sparrows—
a cry, a song, a signal—and knew they ushered in the sun.

You know how the thing that strikes you odd becomes the butt
of jokes, flat and simple like some comic strip: Joe Palooka's
sidekick Knobby Walsh, shifting from black to gray to white

with the intervening years, the Katzenjammer Kids, biff boom
bamm, Batman and the Japs. False clarities. False dawns.
Those other half-formed clarities: groping for the bathroom mirror

at three A.M., to see your shadow as you grip the sink. The shadow
floating in the mirror there, though you stand stock still. The final
recognition of that shadow, those crow's eyes glaring from the glass.

iv

And one, shivering from the wintry drizzle that spattered in that
dank hole, lifted his bent head to meet my unsteady gaze. "What,
are you here, too," I asked him (though he was not), staring now

into his eyes which burned like dying embers, though his cheeks
were streaked with wet. "Hard it is to ask forgiveness, even here,"
I thought I heard him say. "I would forget the past and all

we suffered, though we take it with us into death. That day at table,
when I broke my fist against your face, there where noseridge,
cheekbone and right eye meet, and wore the sling all summer long,

216

it was because the words had failed me. I had a bastard anger
in my heart, had to tell you I was boss and you but one of seven
sparrow mouths all screeling for the worm. When you answered back

I felt your words cut below the waist, and so I struck out as I
had once taught you." And I: "Call it the necessary crossing. I confess
I might have parried by cringing back, but instead I took the blow,

for I am my father's son. Twenty years have come, have gone, since
that day we sat there breaking bread. I have my own sons now
and have known unreasoning anger too. That grayhaired older man,

potbellied and hard of hearing, who put his arms about me crying
when his sister died is not the other one we knew. Strange meeting,
to find you here in my private hell, where I thought to find

myself." And, as I lifted him to kiss him: "Perhaps, my son,
you have." To which I stuttered, wordless, to hold him back,
even as he faded, like panes of ice at last dissolving in the sun.

v

What is it we keep doing to ourselves, our charred tongues
uttering the cleft gutturals? For years haunted by the boy
under the greatlimbed purple beech that fronts my home,

his scrawny arms locked about his knees, sobbing to himself.
When I call to him he does not answer, as if he could not hear.
I see him laced with the gold hush that beech leaves hold

in early spring before they tarnish down to dour purple
like the rest of us. I want to touch him, as though the years
wedged between us like a mirror might somehow melt away.

Strange how his sobbing sounds like singing. I want to comfort him
and have him comfort me, tell him it is all right now and forgive him
his having fathered me. It has come out well I would have him hear.

See: here are my arms, my legs, my eyes, my one good ear, a tongue
that sings. I have splintered into three sons myself, I have
my wife, my friends, my God. Listen: I can sing, though it sound

like crow or sparrow. Let me hold your scrawny shadow in my arms.
And let me forgive you since you could only raise a self from the little
you could know. And though you tasked me hard, it was to flail out

against inertia's darkness, that lovely death, surcease, within.
And though alive now only in my memory, forgive my not becoming all
you wanted, since I had to learn the fact of limitation and, hardest

gift of all, the simple joy of being. Thus, having uttered this,
to cease my years of wrestling with this angel, to call him good
at last and watch him, slowly breaking, embrace the chastened son.

PERMISSIONS AND COPYRIGHTS

223

224

NOTES ON THE POETS
(AND THEIR FATHERS)

WALTER BARGEN is a technical writer and teacher in adult education in central Missouri. His latest book, *The Vertical River* (Timberline Press, 1996), is a sequel to *Yet Other Waters* (1990).

Of his father, he writes: "He died too young, leaving too much for me to ask and too much for me to answer."

WENDY BARKER, born in Summit, New Jersey, now lives in Texas. Her books include: *Let the Ice Speak* (Ithaca House Books/Greenfield Review Press, 1990) and *Lunacy of Light: Emily Dickinson and the Experience of Metaphor* (Southern Illinois University Press, 1987). She has received a Rockefeller Foundation Residency Fellowship and an NEA Creative Writing Fellowship.

"An unwilling banker, my father was a quiet man who read to himself when he came home from work. But sometimes he read poetry out loud to me. He taught me poetry, music, and gardening, and gave me a rose bush of my own when I was eight."

PHYLLIS BECKER was born in Hot Springs, South Dakota, and currently works in social services in Kansas City, Missouri. Some of her poems appear in a chapbook, *Walking Naked Into Sunday* (Wheel of Fire Press, 1995).

"I consider myself lucky, because my father appreciates and understands my poetry because of his love of jazz."

ROBERT BLY, born in Madison, Minnesota, has been a Minnesota resident for most of his life. His influential literary career includes publication of many books of poetry—including *Silence in the Snowy Fields* (1962), *The Teeth Mother Naked at Last* (1970), and *This Tree Will Be Here for a Thousand Years* (1979)—as well as translations from Norwegian, German, and Spanish. His best-selling work, *Iron*

John: A Book About Men (Addison-Wesley, 1990), has recently been followed by another challenge: *The Sibling Society.*

His father was a farmer near Madison, Minnesota.

NEAL BOWERS, a Tennessean by birth, has lived in Ames, Iowa, for twenty years and teaches at Iowa State University. He is author of *Words for the Taking: The Hunt for a Plagiarist* (W. W. Norton, 1997), books on Theodore Roethke, and three volumes of poetry, most recently *Night Vision* (BkMk Press, 1992).

"Even though my dad has been dead for seventeen years, he is astonishingly present in my poems, where I continue to talk and he keeps on listening."

ALAN BRITT, born in Norfolk, Virginia, now lives in Maryland where he edits *Black Moon,* "a literary magazine dedicated to the survival of imagination in U.S. poetry." In addition to several chapbooks, he has published a collection of poetry, *Bodies of Lightning* (CypressBooks, 1995).

"At the age of three months, divorce separated me from my father (now deceased), whom I never met."

GWENDOLYN BROOKS, born in Topeka, Kansas, was raised in Chicago, which has been her home for many years. She is acclaimed as the Poet Laureate of Illinois and has been Poetry Consultant to the Library of Congress. In her distinguished career she has received most of the major awards for poetry, including the Pulitzer Prize and a National Endowment for the Humanities lifetime achievement award.

Gwendolyn Brooks writes of her father: "This man of warm dignity and splendid respectability is the finest man I ever met and I've met four presidents."

OLGA BROUMAS, born in Syros, Greece, now lives in Brewster, Massachusetts, and has published five collections of poetry and three books of translation with Copper Canyon Press.

"My father, Nicholas, was an orphan, raised by his village in the seaside south of Delphi, tending goats and going to school. He later excelled in the military."

DAN BROWN, born and raised in New York City, is author of a poetry collection, *Matter* (Crosstown Books, 1995).

"One of my earliest memories is seeing novels by my father Eugene on the bookshelf at home."

HAYDEN CARRUTH, a New Englander, lived for many years in Vermont and now in Upstate New York. His recent volumes include *Collected Shorter Poems* and *Collected Longer Poems* (from Copper Canyon Press). During his distinguished career he has been editor of *Poetry, Harper's,* and the popular anthology *The Voice That Is Great Within Us.* He has received fellowships from the Bollingen Foundation, Guggenheim Foundation, and the National Endowment for the Arts (Senior Fellowship, 1988).

Hayden Carruth's father, Gorton Veeder Carruth, was a newspaper editor.

RAYMOND CARVER (1938–1988) was born in Clatskanie, Oregon. His books of short fiction include *Cathedral* and *Will You Please Be Quiet, Please?*, which won a National Book Award. He received a National Endowment for the Arts Discovery Award for poetry in 1970. Raymond Carver was living in Port Angeles, Washington, at the time of his death.

His father, Clevie Raymond Carver, worked in lumber mills of Oregon and Washington.

KELLY CHERRY, born in Baton Rouge, Louisiana, teaches at the University of Wisconsin in Madison. Her books include *God's Loud Hand* (Louisiana State University Press, 1993) and a new volume *Death & Transfiguration* (LSU Press, 1997).

"My father was a professor of violin and theory at Louisiana State University. My parents were first and second violinists in string quartets in Ithaca, New York, and Richmond, Virginia."

JOHN CIARDI (1916–1986) was born in Boston. In his distinguished literary career he was an editor of *The Saturday Review,* author of some forty books, including the favorite textbook, *How Does a Poem Mean?,* an internationally acclaimed translator of Dante's *Divine Comedy,* and a popular etymologist with *A Browser's Dictionary* and the entertaining radio column called "A Word in Your Ear."

John Ciardi's parents were immigrants from Italy; his father died when Ciardi was three.

JUDITH ORTIZ COFER, who teaches at the University of Georgia, has published volumes of fiction, essays, and poetry, and has received awards for her work in each genre. A collection of short stories, *An Island Like You: Stories of the Barrio* (Orchard Books, 1995), was named a Best Book of the Year, 1995–96, by the American Library Association.

"I still have a lot to say about my father, but it is coming to me line by line in poems. He died in a car accident in 1976 before I had a chance to ask him all the questions that I must now try to answer through my poetry."

HORACE COLEMAN lives in Huntington Beach, California. He has published poems in several anthologies relating to the Vietnam War, and his chapbook *Between a Rock & a Hard Place* was included in the volume *Four Black Poets* (BkMk Press, 1977).

"My father grew up during the Great Depression and was a WWII vet. He was part of the twentieth-century mass migration of black, Southern, and rural people to the North. He had the brains but not the breaks and was haunted life long by seeing, when he was five, his own father lynched. He knew life aint 'fair' but you still dream, plan, work hard, and 'hustle'—go the extra inch and make supreme efforts. He passed that on."

ELIZABETH COOK-LYNN was born in the Indian hospital at Fort Thompson, South Dakota, and lives in Rapid City. Her publications include *The Power of Horses & Other Stories* (Arcade Publishers, 1991).

"My father was a Santee, born at Sisseton and raised on the Crow Creek, a rodeo rider, a tribal councilman. He raised cattle on the Indian Reservation during hard times and taught his daughters they could be anything they chose to be."

CID CORMAN, born in Boston, has lived and taught in Kyoto, Japan, for many years, where he was also editor and publisher of *Origin* magazine and Origin Press. Many of his numerous poetry books are produced by Origin; other publications include *Plight* (Elizabeth Press, 1969), *Word for Word: Essays on the Art of Language* (Black Sparrow Press, 1977), and a number of translations from the Japanese.

"My father was an exact coeval of Isaac Babel—from the same town—Nikolaev—in the Ukraine—and came to the USA to escape WWI and ended up in the U.S. military instead. He could neither read nor write—but he could manage the horse charts. A born gambler and a wonderful human being."

TOM CRAWFORD, born in Flint, Michigan, currently teaches English in Korea. His books include *If It Weren't for Trees* (Lynx House Press, 1986), *Lauds* (Red Cedar Press, 1993), for which he was honored with an Oregon Book Award, and *China Dancing* (Cedar House Books, 1996).

VANCE CRUMMETT, born in Topeka, Kansas, has studied and taught in Kansas, Missouri, and Wisconsin. A five-year grant from the Abraham Woursell Foundation enabled him to travel in Europe and pursue his studies of literature. He lives in Denver, Colorado, where his daughter, Grace Anna, was born in July, 1996.

"I find myself growing more tolerant of fathers as I become one."

MICHAEL CUDDIHY, a native New Yorker, son and grandson of publishers, turned to poetry in the late sixties and went on to publish *Ironwood* magazine from 1971 to 1988, from his home in Tucson, Arizona. His own books include *A Walled Garden* (Carnegie Mellon University Press, 1989).

"Only when polio landed me in an iron lung at nineteen did I finally come to know my father in all his strengths and weaknesses, an experience that forms the core of my polio memoir, *Man on a Seesaw.*"

BRANDEL FRANCE DE BRAVO, born in Washington, D.C., has published poetry and translations in *The Kenyon Review, Black Warrior Review,* and *TriQuarterly.*

As for her father, she "prefers to let his poem 'The Horde's Prayer' speak for him/her on him: 'For Thine is the Thingdom / and the sour / and the story / forever and never / Ah-Women.'"

RITA DOVE is Commonwealth Professor of English at the University of Virginia in Charlottesville. She was U.S. Poet Laureate from 1993 to 1995, and has published numerous books, among them the Pulitzer-winning poetry collection *Thomas and Beulah* (Carnegie Mellon University Press, 1986).

In Ohio, shortly after her birth in Akron, Rita Dove's father "distinguished himself as the first Black research chemist who broke the race barrier in the tire industry."

JOSEPH DUEMER is the author of *Customs* and *Static,* and coeditor of *Dog Music: Poetry about Dogs* (St. Martin's Press, 1996). He serves as poetry editor for *The Wallace Stevens Journal* and teaches at Clarkson University in Potsdam, New York.

"I never knew either of my fathers."

STEPHEN DUNN was born in Forest Hills, New York. He has published nine books of poetry, including *New and Selected Poems, 1974–1994* (W. W. Norton, 1994), and a volume of essays.

"My father was a salesman, a charming lovely man who did not succeed in business and died in his late fifties."

CORNELIUS EADY's poetry books, which include *You Don't Miss Your Water* (Henry Holt and Co., 1995) and *The Autobiography of a Jukebox* (Carnegie Mellon University Press, 1996), have won him many awards, including a Guggenheim Fellowship and a Rockefeller Foundation Fellowship to Bellagio, Italy. He currently teaches and directs the Poetry Center at SUNY-Stony Brook, New York.

"My father grew up in the Tampa, Florida, area . . . moved to Rochester, New York, where he worked first as a construction worker, and then joined the City of Rochester, where he worked for the Water Dept. He died three years ago. I am named for him and his father, Robert, who I believe, owned his own land."

DAVE ETTER was born in California and has lived most of his life in the Middle West. He has published twenty-four books of poetry, including *Sunflower County* and *Carnival,* both from Spoon River Press.

"My father and I had very little in common but we always treated each other with love and respect."

DAVID ALLAN EVANS, born in Sioux City, Iowa, now lives in Brookings, South Dakota. He has published three books of poems, including *Hanging Out With the Crows* (BkMk Press, 1991) and, with his wife Jan, *Double Happiness: Two Lives in China* (University of South Dakota Press, 1995).

His father died in 1963.

CHARLES FISHMAN was born in Oceanside, New York; he now lives in Wantagh and teaches at the State University of New York in Farmingdale. His recent poetry book is *The Firewalkers* (Avisson Press, 1996) and he is editor of the anthology, *Blood to Remember: American Poets on the Holocaust* (Texas Tech University Press, 1991).

"My father, Murray, worked as a color chemist for a printing ink plant in New York City and has been a lifelong fisherman."

ROBERT GIBB, a Pennsylvanian, returned to Pittsburgh in 1992 with his wife and two sons. His poetry books include *The Winter House* and *Fugue for a Late Snow* (both from University of Missouri Press, 1984 and 1993).

"I pursue a phantom markedly like the figure in the poem 'The Race,' which seems at times still to be within reach, and then turns ethereal once more. Stevens writes of a 'race of fathers,' the last of which is air. In his silent and wounded presence, my father was elemental like that."

GARY GILDNER is author of several poetry books, including *Blue Like the Heavens* (University of Pittsburgh Press, 1984), a novel, a collection of short stories, and a memoir, *The Warsaw Sparks* (University of Iowa Press, 1990), which tells about the year he lived in Poland and coached a Polish baseball team.

"I was born in West Branch, Michigan, as was my father, Ted, who was a carpenter."

MARIA MAZZIOTTI GILLAN's latest book is *Where I Come From* (Guernica, 1995). With her daughter, Jennifer, she edited *Unsettling America* (Viking Penguin, 1994). She is Director of the Poetry Center at Passaic County Community College in New Jersey.

"Arturo Mazziotti immigrated from southern Italy to Paterson in 1922 when he was sixteen years old; he worked at odd jobs and as an unskilled worker in the silk mills. He served as an orator for Italian social and political events. Though he is fascinated by American politics, at ninety, he still speaks very little English."

LOUISE GLÜCK, born in New York City, edited *The Best American Poetry* (Collier Books, 1993), and her own poetry books include *The House on Marshland* and *The Wild Iris* (Ecco Press, 1975, 1992). She has received a prize from *Poetry* magazine, and Fellowships from the National Endowment for the Arts and the Guggenheim Foundation, among other awards.

ALBERT GOLDBARTH lives in Wichita, Kansas. His collection *Heaven and Earth: a Cosmology* received the National Book Critics Circle Award, and has been followed by numerous other collections—most recently, *Adventures in Ancient Egypt* (Ohio State University Press).

"My lower-middle-class insurance salesman father wasn't a reader of *any* kind, much less a reader of poetry. But he came from that 'first generation' of American Jews that intuitively valued 'book learning,' and he loved to see the family name on the spine of a volume. I believe that, in his own uncomprehending but sweetly supportive way, he hovers benignly over an anthology like this, invisibly cheering, kvetching, and enthusing, as he did in life."

PAUL GOODMAN (1911–1972), born in New York City, is known internationally for his works of social criticism, especially *Growing Up Absurd,* and for *Gestalt Therapy.* He also wrote avant-garde novels—*The Empire City*—and poetry. He taught at the University of Chicago, New York University, Black Mountain College, and other places, and traveled widely to lecture.

Goodman's father abandoned the family while Paul was still an infant.

WILLIAM GREENWAY is Distinguished Professor of English at Youngstown State University. His fifth collection of poetry is *How the Dead Bury the Dead* (University of Akron Press, 1994).

"I was born and raised in Atlanta, Georgia, where my father was a Southern Baptist minister. He was a gentle and spiritual, strong and opinionated man who died far too young and thinking himself a failure. Our complicated relationship continues.

RACHEL HADAS, born in New York City, is the author of eleven books of essays, translations, and poetry, including *Mirrors of Astonishment* and *Other Worlds Than This* (Rutgers University Press, 1992, 1994). She teaches at the Newark campus of Rutgers University, and has also taught at Columbia and Princeton.

"My father, Moses Hadas, a distinguished classical scholar, died in 1966."

SAM HAMILL has published more than thirty volumes of poetry (including translations from ancient Greek, Chinese, Japanese, Latin, and Estonian) and essays. He is editor at Copper Canyon Press in Port Townsend, Washington.

"I was orphaned during World War II and adopted by a Utah farm family in 1946."

ROBERT HAYDEN (1913–1980), born in Detroit, was at Fisk University for twenty-three years and then a Professor of English at the University of Michigan. He also served as Poetry Consultant to the Library of Congress and was a member of the American Academy and Institute of Arts and Letters. His books ranged from *Heart Shape in the Dust* (1940) to *Angle of Ascent: New and Selected Poems* (Liveright, 1975).

JONATHAN HOLDEN is Professor of English and Poet-in-Residence at Kansas State University, Manhattan. His books include *The Names of the Rapids* (University of Massachusetts Press, 1985) and *American Gothic* (University of Georgia Press, 1992).

"My father, Alan Nordby Holden (1904–1985), was a crystalographer for the Bell Telephone Laboratories in Murray Hill, New Jersey."

DAVID IGNATOW, born in Brooklyn, has lived in New York City most of his life (and now on Long Island). After a business career with a bindery, Ignatow taught at many colleges, and has published numerous volumes of poetry and prose. He has received the Bollingen Prize, Guggenheim Fellowships, the Shelley Memorial, and served as president of the Poetry Society of America.

David Ignatow has written extensively of his relationship with his father, who was an immigrant from Russia and a bookbinder.

COLETTE INEZ lives in New York City and has published seven books of poetry, including *Getting Underway: New and Selected Poetry* and *Family Life* (Story Line Press). She teaches at Columbia University's Writing Program, General Studies.

"I was born in Brussels, Belgium, in the year my father was ordained a Monsignor of the Roman Catholic Church."

WILL INMAN, born in Wilmington, North Carolina, is now retired, living and writing in Tucson.

"My father, William Archibald McGirt, Sr. (I was born Jr.), was a pioneer roads-and-bridges visionary in southeastern North Carolina."

RICHARD JONES teaches at DePaul University in Chicago. His three poetry volumes from Copper Canyon Press are *Country of Air, At Last We Enter Paradise,* and *A Perfect Time.*

"I was born in London, England, where my father, an Air Force pilot, was stationed after the war. In April, 1996, he flew to Chicago, where together we celebrated his eightieth birthday."

DONALD JUSTICE, born in Miami, Florida, received the Pulitzer Prize in 1980 for his *Selected Poems* (Atheneum). He has published *A Donald Justice Reader* (1991) and a *New and Selected Poems* (Alfred A. Knopf, 1995). He has been a Professor at the University of Iowa and the University of Florida.

His family was originally from south Georgia, and his father was a carpenter.

LAWRENCE KEARNEY, born in Oxford, England, grew up in Buffalo, New York. He now lives in the Boston area with his wife, Karen, and their two children, and works as an antique dealer. His first book was *Kingdom Come* (Wesleyan University Press, 1980).

"My Scottish father, who died last year, could be scathingly funny, brutal, sentimental, insanely enraged by the smallest infraction, a wonderful musician, and worked like a donkey most of his life."

GALWAY KINNELL, born in Providence, Rhode Island, divides his time between New York City and Vermont, has taught poetry at many universities in this country and in France and Australia. His *Selected Poems* won both the National Book Award and the Pulitzer Prize in 1982, and he has been the recipient of a MacArthur Fellowship. He is Samuel F. B. Morse Professor of Arts and Science at New York University.

CAROLYN KIZER, born in Spokane, Washington, is author of seven books of poetry, including *The Nearness of You* and *Mermaids in the Basement* (both from Copper Canyon Press), and two books of essays. She was the founding editor of *Poetry Northwest*, director of literary programs for the National Endowment for the Arts in the 1960s, and has taught in writing programs around the country.

"I am the only daughter of Benjamin Kizer, lawyer and planner. He was fifty when I was born, and lived to be one hundred."

ETHERIDGE KNIGHT (1931–1991), born in Corinth, Mississippi, published his *Poems from Prison* in 1968, followed by *Belly Song* (Broadside Press) and a collection he edited called *Black Voices from Prison*. A roundup collection of his work was published as *The Essential Etheridge Knight* (University of Pittsburgh Press, 1986), and he received many literary awards. Etheridge Knight was a popular presence on poetry reading circuits.

He was named after his father, Etheridge "Bushie" Knight, who had seven children.

YUSEF KOMUNYAKAA's latest book, *Neon Vernacular* (Wesleyan University Press, 1993), was awarded both the Pulitzer Prize and the Kingsley Tufts Award in 1994. That same year he also received the William Faulkner Prize from the Université de Rennes. He teaches at Princeton University.

"I was born in Bogalusa, Louisiana. My father was a finishing carpenter, and I feel that his precision taught me a lot about the craft of poetry. 'My Father's Loveletters' seems to be informed by condemnation and praise."

MAXINE KUMIN won a Pulitzer Prize in 1973, the Poets' Prize in 1993, was Consultant in Poetry to the Library of Congress, and is now a Chancellor of the Academy of American Poets. Her most recent book of poems is *Connecting the Dots* (W. W. Norton, 1996).

"I was born in Philadelphia, Pennsylvania, the daughter of Peter Winokur, a pawnbroker who worked long hours six days a week and rested so hard on the seventh that he invariably exclaimed on Sunday night, 'Well, I murdered this day.'"

GREG KUZMA, born in Rome, New York, teaches in Lincoln, Nebraska, and has been published widely: his new long poems are appearing in *TriQuarterly, Harvard Review, Poetry East, Iowa Review,* and elsewhere.

"My father Harry died in 1991. I have written two books (unpublished) about him, one based on his 'famous sayings.'"

ELAINE LALLY has worked in college libraries in Kansas and Missouri for a number of years. She divides her time between Overland Park, Kansas, and Powell in southern Missouri.

"I was born in Effingham, Illinois. At age twelve, while living in San Francisco—and with only one employment clue—I tracked down my father in Chicago."

LI-YOUNG LEE was born in Jakarta, Indonesia, of Chinese parents, and now lives in Chicago. His books of poetry include *The City in Which I Love You* and *Rose* (BOA Editions) and *The Winged Seed* (Simon & Schuster, 1995). He received the 1994 Lavan Younger Poet Award from The Academy of American Poets.

Li-Young Lee's father fled with his family from Indonesia, where he had been held as a political prisoner.

MIA LEONIN, born in Kansas City and raised in Marshall, Missouri, received her Master of Fine Arts from the University of Miami. Now residing in Miami, she is working on her first collection of poetry.

"My father came to the United States from Havana, Cuba, in 1963."

PHILIP LEVINE, born in Detroit of Russian-Jewish immigrant parents, has lived and taught in Fresno for many years. His *New Selected Poems* (Alfred A. Knopf, 1991) includes poems from his award-winning books—*7 Years from Somewhere,* National Book Critics Circle Award, and *Ashes,* American Book Award, and many other titles.

"The war my father is fleeing in the poem ["Late Light"] is WWI; he served for some years with the British army in Palestine. The war my son was fleeing was the war of his generation, in Vietnam."

EDWARD C. LYNSKEY, born in Arlington, Virginia, has published book reviews in *The New York Times* and *The Washington Post*, and his poetry has appeared in *The Atlantic Monthly, American Poetry Review,* and *New Letters.*

"My father is a big fan of Hank Williams." (See poem.)

MARJORIE MADDOX originally from Columbus, Ohio, teaches English at Lock Haven University in Pennsylvania. Her poetry has been widely published, and her book, *Perpendicular As I,* received the Sandstone Publishing's 1994 Poetry Award.

"My newest manuscript, *Transplant, Transport, Transubstantiation,* focuses on my father's unsuccessful heart transplant during the '93 blizzard."

PAUL MARIANI, like his father before him, was born in New York City. He is Distinguished University Professor at the University of Massachusetts/Amherst, and his publications include a biography, *William Carlos Williams: A New World Naked.* He is married to Eileen Spinosa and is the father of three sons.

"My father, also Paul Mariani, served in the U.S. Army during WWII, was a mechanic and foreman until his retirement, and the father of seven children."

PETER MARKUS was born in Mt. Clemens, Michigan, and now lives in Detroit.

"Many of my earliest memories of my father revolve around his hands: the gripping of tools, the turning of nuts and screws, working late out in the garage with his hunched-over body half swallowed by the open hood of his '73 T-Bird. And now, when I look at my own hands, I see my father's hands that seem strangely unfit and uncomfortable when holding something so small as a pen."

WALTER McDONALD is author of sixteen collections of poems and stories, including *Counting Survivors* (University of Pittsburgh Press, 1995), *After the Noise of Saigon* (University of Massachusetts Press), *Night Landings* (HarperCollins), and three that won Western Heritage Awards from the National Cowboy Hall of Fame. He is Paul Whitfield Horn Professor of English and Director of Creative Writing at Texas Tech University.

"My dad served in World War I and then for years as a working cowboy, big-knuckled and patient, and I learned from him the tough, hard facts of work and the value of family."

COLLEEN J. McELROY teaches in the English Department at the University of Washington in Seattle. She has published collections of poetry and short stories (including *Driving Under the Cardboard Pines* and *What Madness Brought Me Here: New and Selected Poems, 1968–88*), and writes for stage and television. She has been awarded fellowships from the Fulbright Foundation, the National Endowment for the Arts, and the Rockefeller Foundation.

"My father was career Army, retired in 1964 after twenty-five years of service. He loves his daughter despite her views of the military."

RON McFARLAND, born in Bellaire, Ohio, and raised in Cocoa, Florida, now teaches at the University of Idaho (and, after twenty-six years, thinks of himself as an Idahoan). His most recent book of poetry is *The Haunting Familiarity of Things* (Singular Speech Press, 1993).

"As an Air Force captain at the end of World War II my father passed up the golden opportunities of the GI Bill and opted for a steady but unexciting job with a hardware wholesaler. He has always had a deep sense of 'family,' and has never been one to look back with regret. As a man and father, I have been more self-centered, and I suspect that when *I* am eighty-one years old, I will not be able to feel as serene or as certain that I have done the right thing as he seems to be."

MICHAEL McIRVIN, born in Sidney, Nebraska, now lives in Cheyenne, Wyoming. His two collections of poetry are *Love and Myth* and *Lessons of Radical Finitude*.

"At this point in life, forty, I am trying to figure out what it is to be a good father—I have two young sons—but also a good son within the constraints of who my father is, what he is, and what he can't be—both before it's too late."

STEVE MILES teaches at Colorado State University and lives in Denver with an "adopted" family of his own.

"I was born in Oklahoma City where my first father left the family. Jim Miles then adopted me and my two brothers and one sister."

PHILIP MILLER, born in Kansas City, Missouri, teaches at Kansas City, Kansas, Community College. His books of poetry include *Hard Freeze* (BkMk Press, 1995) and *From the Temperate Zone* (with Keith Denniston, Potpourri Press, 1996). He directs the River Front Readings Series in Kansas City.

"My father, Richard McChesney Miller, was a visual artist, poet, and opera singer and introduced me to all of the arts, for which I am eternally grateful."

ALAN NAPIER, of Brimfield, Ohio, has published poems in *The American Poetry Review*, the anthology *Atomic Ghost*, and elsewhere. His computer art has been shown in *Computer Artist*, on CD rom, on calendars, and has been exhibited both in the United States and Europe.

LORINE NIEDECKER (1903–1970) was born in Fort Atkinson, Wisconsin. She worked in a library, a hospital, and a radio station, and her publications include *From This Condensery: The Complete Writing of Lorine Niedecker* (Jargon Society, 1985). A new *Selected Poems: The Granite Pail*, edited by Cid Corman, was published by Gnomon Press, 1996, and a revised *Collected Poems* is forthcoming from the University of California Press.

Lorine Niedecker's father was a carp seiner around the Blackhawk Island area of Wisconsin, and many references to his occupation appear in her poems.

ED OCHESTER's most recent book of poems is *Allegheny* (Adastra Press, 1995). He is director of the writing program at the University of Pittsburgh and editor of the Pitt Poetry Series.

"My father was a hard-working and 'self-made' man who grew up in poverty in Brooklyn, supported his mother and two younger brothers when he graduated from high school, married late for economic reasons, and was not happy when his only son (the first person in the family to graduate from college) did not attend law school."

SIMON J. ORTIZ was born in Albuquerque, New Mexico, and raised on the Acoma Pueblo Indian Reservation west of there. His books of stories and poems include *Going for the Rain* (Harper, 1976) and *Woven Stone* (University of Arizona Press, 1991).

"Although at times troublesome—what father isn't at times?—my father and the place he represented in Indian culture has been a significant influence on my poetry."

LINDA PASTAN is author of nine books of poems, including *An Early Afterlife* (W. W. Norton, 1995) and *Heroes in Disguise* (Norton, 1991). She lives in Potomac, Maryland.

"I was born in New York City where my father was a surgeon. *An Early Afterlife* contains a number of poems about him."

KARL PATTEN, born in Beverly, Massachusetts, teaches at Bucknell University, Pennsylvania. He is author of *The Impossible Reaches* (Dorcas Press) and coeditor of *West Branch*.

"For all his working life, my father was a milliner, with a reputation as a kind of genius in design, in Boston."

MOLLY PEACOCK, author of four collections of poetry, including *Take Heart* (Random House, 1989) and *Original Love* (W. W. Norton, 1996), is an editor of *Poetry in Motion: 100 Poems from the Subways and Buses* and a contributing writer for *House & Garden.*

"I was born in Buffalo, New York, where my hard-drinking father, a veteran of the U.S. Navy, worked all his life as an electrician for the Niagara Mohawk Power Co."

ERSKINE PETERS, born in Augusta, Georgia, is presently Professor of English and African-American Studies at the University of Notre Dame. His poems have appeared in *Obsidian II, Common Sense, Xavier Review,* and elsewhere.

"My father was named George Raymond Peters, Sr. He was a World War II veteran and died in 1988."

ROBERT PETERS, who grew up in Northern Wisconsin, lives in Huntington Beach, California. He has published over thirty collections of poetry, including *Songs for a Son* (W. W. Norton, 1967) and *Poems Selected and New, 1967–1991* (Asylum Arts, 1992). His volumes of criticism include *Where the Bee Sucks: Workers, Drones and Queens of Contemporary American Poetry* (Asylum Arts, 1994).

"My father, a mechanic and farmer, had no formal education, taught himself to play numerous musical instruments, finally owned a small welding shop, and was always proud of Robert, his oldest son."

ANTHONY PETROSKY was born in Exeter, Pennsylvania, into a family of miners, farmers, and carpenters. His first book, *Jurgis Petraskas,* received the Walt Whitman Award, and his second is *Red and Yellow Boat* (Louisiana State University, 1994).

"My father, Anthony, lives by himself in Buffalo, New York, where he is retired from twenty-five years on the line at General Motors."

ROBERT PHILLIPS is author of five books of poetry, including *Breakdown Lane* (Johns Hopkins University Press), which was a finalist for the 1995 Poets' Prize and a *New York Times* "Notable Book of the Year." He is Professor of English at the University of Houston.

"My father, T. Allen Phillips, was a metallurgical engineer and a high school chemistry and physics teacher."

STANLEY PLUMLY's first book, *In the Outer Dark*, won the Delmore Schwartz Memorial Award. His newest collection of poems is *The Marriage in the Trees* (Ecco Press, 1996). He teaches at the University of Maryland.

Stanley Plumly was born in Barnesville, Ohio, and has said that a great many of his poems relate in some way to his father, an alcoholic.

DAN QUISENBERRY from Santa Monica, now living in Leawood, Kansas, is an ex baseball pitcher for the Kansas City Royals, the St. Louis Cardinals, and the San Francisco Giants. He now plays at lots of other stuff, including poetry. A chapbook, *Down and In*, was published as a Helicon Nine Editions *feuillet* in 1995.

"My father is a hard-working, hard-playing man who has discovered golf."

MARGARET RANDALL, born in New York, spent twenty-five years in Latin America—Mexico, Cuba, Nicaragua—and now lives in Albuquerque, New Mexico. Her books include *Dancing With the Doe* (West End Press, 1991), *The Price You Pay: The Hidden Cost of Women's Relationship to Money,* and *Hunger's Table* (Papier-Maché Press, 1997).

"My father, John Randall, died of Alzheimer's in 1994. I write a great deal about him and about us."

DAVID RAY's books of poetry include *Kangaroo Paws: Poems Written in Australia* (Thomas Jefferson University Press, 1995) and *Wool Highways* (Helicon Nine Editions, 1993), which won the William Carlos Williams Award from the Poetry Society of America. Several of his articles have appeared in *The New York Times Magazine,* and a memoir is being published by Dutton/Signet.

"I saw my father very few times after the divorce of my parents, when I was about eight. My father was a barber, who served in World War II and set up shop in Long Beach, California, where he died a few years ago."

JUDY RAY, born and raised on a farm in southern England, has traveled widely and lived in the United States since 1969. Her books include a prose memoir, *The Jaipur Sketchbook: Impressions of India,* and *Pigeons in the Chandeliers,* poems. She was Director of The Writers Place in Kansas City for its first three years, 1992–95.

"My father, Wilfrid T. H. Morrish, was a farmer in Sussex, England, until his death at age eighty-seven. He believed in the 'work ethic,' was a Methodist lay preacher, enjoyed telling jokes, and never traveled outside England, except to cross the Severn River into Wales."

SHREELA RAY was born in India and came to the United States in the early 1960s. She lived in Upstate New York, and her book of poems, *Night Conversations with None Other*, was published by Dustbooks in 1977.

F. D. REEVE, born in Philadelphia, Pennsylvania, now lives in Vermont and teaches at Wesleyan University. His poetry books include *The Blue Cat* and *Concrete Music;* he has also published several novels, a volume of short stories, (*A Few Rounds of Old Maid*, 1995), and many translations from Russian. His awards include fellowships from the Ingram-Merrill Foundation and the Rockefeller Foundation.

"My father was a witty, macho outdoors type who loved comfort and connections; a good shot, a fine fisherman."

TRISH REEVES, born in Columbia, Missouri, teaches at Haskell Indian Nations University in Lawrence, Kansas. She has received a National Endowment for the Arts Fellowship, been a Yaddo Fellow, and won the Cleveland State University Poetry Center Prize for her book, *Returning the Question* (1988).

"I was born during my father's last year of law school, and was fortunate to have the first nine months of life with a somewhat-available father (before he disappeared into an ethical practice of law); reportedly, he would feed me when my mother was no longer willing to."

DAISY RHAU was born in Los Angeles, California. She is an MFA candidate at Penn State University where she holds the Katey Lehman fellowship.

"My father is a Presbyterian minister, now volunteering as a pastoral care chaplain, counseling the terminally ill at various Los Angeles hospitals."

LEN ROBERTS is the author of eight books of poetry, including *Counting the Black Angels* (University of Illinois Press, 1989).

"I was born in Cohoes, New York, to Margery Roberts, a textile mill worker, and Raymond Roberts, a bread deliveryman for Golden Eagle Bakery. At the age of twenty-eight, in an attempt to communicate with my father who had been dead for six years, I wrote what turned out to be my first poems. My father is still my 'muse,' the one whom I turn to for the right words."

WILLIAM PITT ROOT was born in Austin, Minnesota, and raised near the Everglades. His most recent work, the chapter he contributed to *Heatstroke: A Collabo-*

rative Novel (Fall, 1996), follows *Trace Elements from a Recurring Kingdom* (Confluence, 1994) which gathers his first five books.

"Here's the opening of a poem [about my father] I've never finished: '*Street Angel, House Devil,* / that's what your mother called you, / and your wife knew why.'"

LARRY RUBIN teaches English at Georgia Tech in Atlanta. His poetry has been widely published in the major literary magazines, including *The New Yorker, Harper's Magazine, Poetry, The Nation,* etc.; his books include *All My Mirrors Lie* (David R. Godine, 1975) and *The World's Old Way* (University of Nebraska Press, 1963).

"I was born in Bayonne, New Jersey. My father was a pioneer pharmacist in the then-small town of Miami Beach, Florida, where we moved in 1932, and where I grew up."

MARK RUDMAN was born in New York City and grew up in the care of his mother and her rabbi husband in the Midwest and West. His book-length poem *Rider* (Wesleyan University Press) received the National Book Critics Circle Award for 1994 and his sequel, *The Millennium Hotel,* appeared in 1996.

"My father was often great to be around when he wasn't drunk, and he died, having become depressed in his mid-seventies, by jumping from an eleventh story terrace in a place where he didn't want to be: Miami."

BIFF RUSS, born in Montague, Massachusetts, now lives in Evanston, Illinois. Her first book, *Black Method* (Helicon Nine Editions, 1991), won the Marianne Moore Poetry Prize.

"My father, Harry Earle Russ, also a native of Massachusetts, was a U.S. Navy veteran stationed in China during WWII. He worked most of the rest of his life for the Boston and Maine Railroad. He died at the age of sixty-six from emphysema."

BENJAMIN ALIRE SÁENZ, born in Old Picacho, New Mexico, teaches at the University of Texas at El Paso. His first book of poems, *Calendar of Dust* (1991), won a Before Columbus American Book Award, and other publications include *Flowers for the Broken* (stories) and *Carry Me Like Water* (a novel). He received a Lannan Poetry Fellowship in 1993.

HARVEY SHAPIRO is author of several poetry volumes published by Wesleyan University Press, and his *Selected Poems* will be published by Carcanet Press in

1997. He has had a forty-year editorial career with magazines and newspapers, including *Commentary, The New Yorker, The New York Times Book Review,* and *The New York Times Magazine.*

"On my Chicago birth certificate, my father listed himself as an attorney, though he had never graduated from high school. I figure he wanted to give me a better start in life."

RICHARD SHELTON, born in Boise, Idaho, is author of *Selected Poems: 1969–1981* (University of Pittsburgh Press) and *Going Back to Bisbee* (University of Arizona Press), which won the Western States Award for Creative Nonfiction in 1992. He is Regents Professor in the English Department at the University of Arizona.

"The poem ['Job the Father'] has nothing to do with my father. It is about my relationship to my son, who was born at Ft. Huachuca, Arizona."

CHARLES SIMIC, born in Yugoslavia, lives in Strafford, N.H., and teaches at the University of New Hampshire. His many volumes of poetry include *The Book of Gods and Devils* and *A Wedding in Hell* (Harcourt Brace, 1990 and 1994), and he has translated the work of many Yugoslavian poets. He has been the recipient of the Pulitzer Prize as well as awards from the American Academy of Arts and Letters and the Guggenheim Foundation.

His father, George Simic, was an engineer who worked for a telephone company in the Chicago area.

FLOYD SKLOOT, born in Brooklyn, New York, now lives in Amity, Oregon. His most recent books are *Music Appreciation*, poetry (University Press of Florida, 1994) and *Summer Blue*, a novel, (Story Line Press, 1994).

"My father, a poultry butcher who briefly worked in the women's fashion business after selling his chicken market, died in 1961."

MBEMBE MILTON SMITH (1947–1982) was a Kansas City poet, author of four chapbooks, including *Allegory of the Bebop Walk* (in *Four Black Poets*, BkMk Press, 1977) and a *Selected Poems* (published posthumously by BkMk Press, 1983). Mbembe's death in Chicago in 1982, ruled a suicide, cut short a promising future.

Mrs. Samella Myers Gates, Mbembe's mother, writes of his father: "Oscar W. Smith (1915–1971), native of Abilene, Texas, was also father of four other sons. An only child, proud of his sons, he lived in Texas, Nebraska, and Iowa and, after separation within the marriage, arranged for summer visits for his sons from about 1953 to 1963."

JASON SOMMER, born in New York City, has lived in Ireland, where he taught at University College, Dublin, and reviewed for the *Irish Independent.* His new book of poems, *Other People's Troubles,* will be published by University of Chicago Press in 1997. He teaches literature and creative writing at Fontbonne College in St. Louis, Missouri.

"My father is a Holocaust survivor, former National Teacher of the Year, and author of the memoir, *Journey to the Golden Door: A Survivor's Tale* (Shengold Publishers, N.Y.)."

KIM R. STAFFORD's books of poetry include *A Gypsy's History of the World, The Granary, Places & Stories,* and *Braided Apart.* He lives in Portland, Oregon, where he is Director of The Northwest Writing Institute at Lewis & Clark College.

His father was the well-known poet, William Stafford, with whom Kim collaborated on a number of projects, including the book *Braided Apart.*

WILLIAM STAFFORD (1914–1993) was born in Hutchinson, Kansas, and served as a conscientious objector during World War II, and taught at Lewis & Clark College from 1948 to 1980. His book *Traveling Through the Dark* won a National Book Award in 1963. He died at his home in Oregon in 1993.

A note from son Kim Stafford says: "His own father carried copies of poems in his wallet to read, during his work on the road."

ROBERT STEWART, born in St. Louis, is author of *Plumbers* (poems, BkMk Press) and *Letter from the Living* (poems and an essay, Borderline). His poems have appeared in *Stand, Denver Quarterly, Poetry Northwest,* and elsewhere. He teaches at the University of Missouri-Kansas City and is also Managing Editor of *New Letters.*

"My father is a retired plumber and a former official for the International Association of Plumbers and Pipefitters, a trade union."

CAROLE STONE is Professor of English at Montclair State University, N.J., and author of three poetry chapbooks. She has received four Fellowships from the New Jersey State Council on the Arts.

"I was born in Newark, New Jersey, where my father owned a nightclub."

RUTH STONE was born in Roanoke, Virginia, in a stone house built by her grandfather. She now lives in Binghamton, New York, and a collection of her poems, *Second-Hand Coat: Poems New and Selected,* was published in 1987.

"My father was a musician and played drums (in jazz and symphony orchestras) and influenced my work—unwittingly—by playing drums at home—he built rhythms into my mind."

TERESE SVOBODA's most recent books include *Mere Mortals* (poetry) and *Cannibal* (fiction). She currently lives in New York City.

"My father, Frank B. Svoboda, farms and ranches and lawyers throughout southwest Nebraska where I was born and raised."

JOHN TAGLIABUE, born near Lake Como in Italy, came to America when he was four. He has taught at universities around the world, including Lebanon, Italy, Spain, Greece, Brazil, Indonesia, China, and Japan, as well as regularly at Bates College, Maine. His five poetry books include *The Great Day* (Alembic Press), and a *Collected Poems, 1941–96* will be published in 1997.

"My father was energetic and generous, serving as host in his good New Jersey Italian restaurants; and during his last fifteen years (partly paralyzed) near our house in Maine he was an inspiration for me."

JAMES TATE, born in Kansas City, Missouri, now teaches at the University of Massachusetts. An early book, *The Lost Pilot* (1967), was selected for the Yale Series of Younger Poets and his many other volumes of poetry have also been received with acclaim, including the *Selected Poems,* for which he received the Pulitzer Prize.

WILLIAM TROWBRIDGE is Distinguished Professor at Northwest Missouri State University where, in addition to teaching, he coedits *The Laurel Review*/Greentower Press. His poetry books include *Enter Dark Stranger* and *O Paradise* (University of Arkansas Press, 1989 and 1995).

"I was born in Chicago. My father was a World War II combat veteran and a corporation executive who died in 1989 of Alzheimer's disease and lung cancer."

MARTIN TUCKER, born to Russian immigrants, is editor of the literary journal *Confrontation,* on the Executive Board of PEN American Center, and author of several literary studies and criticism, including *Sam Shephard* and *Africa in Modern*

Literature. A new poetry collection is *Attention Spans* (Potpourri Publications, Kansas, 1996).

"My father, a poet by temperament, worked as an electrician for the Brooklyn Navy Yard, among other venues."

PAMELA USCHUK's collection of poetry, *Without Birds, Without Flowers, Without Trees,* is in its fourth printing. Recipient of several national poetry awards, Pamela Uschuk currently teaches poetry workshops on Native American reservations in Arizona through Arts Reach.

"My father, George Uschuk, son of a Russian immigrant, was a decorated war veteran who fought in both European and South Pacific theaters."

GLORIA VANDO is a Nuyorican living in Kansas City, where she publishes Helicon Nine Editions. Her poetry has won several awards, including the 1994 Thorpe Menn Award for her first book, *Promesas: Geography of the Impossible* (Arte Publico Press), two Billee Murray Denny Prizes, and a Kansas Arts Commission Fellowship in poetry.

"My father was a chemist who worked for the Henry Heide Candy Company and wrote poems on the company stationery. He was also a journalist, playwright, actor, and political activist in New York City and Puerto Rico."

JUDITH VOLLMER's first book, *Level Green* (University of Wisconsin Press, 1990), won the Brittingham Prize. Born in Pittsburgh, Vollmer is also the recipient of a 1993 National Endowment for the Arts Fellowship.

"My father, Regis, worked among the 1950s–1970s nuclear industry technicians inside reactors in the United States and Europe; he is a gardener and devoted grandfather."

RONALD WALLACE's nine books of poetry include *Time's Fancy, The Makings of Happiness,* and *People and Dog in the Sun* (all published by the University of Pittsburgh Press). He directs the creative writing program at the University of Wisconsin and edits the University of Wisconsin Press poetry series. He divides his time between Madison and a forty-acre farm in Bear Valley, Wisconsin.

"I worried about 'using' my father and his illness in my poetry; he said, 'I've felt so useless to anyone for so long that if I can be of use to you in this it would make me happy.'"

MICHAEL S. WEAVER, born in Baltimore, Maryland, now lives in Massachusetts. His books include *My Father's Geography* and *Timber and Prayer* (University of Pittsburgh Press, 1992 and 1995).

"My father and I often talk about baseball and the old world."

ROBERT WINNER, born in the Bronx in 1930, was a stockbroker, vice president of a leading securities firm, and then president of Lakewood, New Jersey, Cemetery Association. His books include *Green in the Body* (Slow Loris Press, 1979), *Flogging the Czar* (The Sheep Meadow Press, 1983), and *The Sanity of Earth and Grass* (Tilbury House, 1994).

DAVID WOJAHN was born in St. Paul, Minnesota, and now lives in Bloomington, where he teaches at Indiana University. The most recent of his four collections of poetry is *Late Empire* (University of Pittsburgh Press, 1994).

"My father worked for thirty years for the Great Northern Railroad."

NANCY MEANS WRIGHT divides her time between Vermont and New York. She has been a Bread Loaf Scholar and has published poems in many literary magazines. Her third novel, *Mad Season*, was published by St. Martin's Press in 1996.

"I was born in New Jersey to a funloving, Scots-Irish tenor."

QIU XIAOLONG, born in Shanghai, China, now lives in St. Louis, Missouri.

"Of course a poet's father does not have to be the father in the poem. Often, in another land, I wish there could be such a stamp [see Qiu Xialong's poem] to mail me to him."

PAUL ZIMMER was born in Canton, Ohio. He has published a dozen books and chapbooks of poetry, including *Big Blue Train* (University of Arkansas Press, 1994) and *The Great Bird of Love* (University of Illinois Press, 1989). He is Director of the University of Iowa Press in Iowa City.

"My father was a fine and human influence on my life and I loved him very much."

PAUL ZWEIG (1935–1984) was born in New York City and taught at Queens College. His poetry books include *Eternity's Woods* and *The Dark Side of the Earth;* he is also author of *Walt Whitman: The Making of the Poet,* and an autobiography, *Three Journeys: An Automythology.*

INDEX OF POETS